"*The Heart and Soul of Parish Ministry* is an extraordinarily valuable book, at once profound and down-to earth. It is the fruit of years of pastoral experience and thoughtful reflection on the mission and ministries of the Church. Regina Coll has been a lifelong parishoner, a teacher, and a director of field education for women and men preparing for various ministries in the Church.

This book touches every major topic of interest and concern to present and future ministers, and it is the touch of someone who has been gifted with marvelously rich spiritual and pastoral insights. It should be required reading for ministerial students, for members of parish staffs, and indeed for everyone who aspires to derive maximum spiritual benefit from parish life."

Richard P. McBrien,
Crowley-O'Brien Professor of Theology
University of Notre Dame

"In measured and inspired language, veteran teacher Regina Coll takes us through the practical theology and spirituality of ecclesial lay ministry. It couldn't come at a better time now that we've been at it a few years. I can see this book both as required reading for those currently in lay ministry formation programs and for those already in the field. I recommend *The Heart and Soul of Parish Ministry* to all."

William J. Bausch
Author, *The Total Parish Manual* and *Brave New Church*

"This is a beautiful book, rich in lore and in the stories of our faith. The particular force that struck me in reading it was that it deepened and heightened the tradition on every page: Eucharist, community, artistic forms, history, and faith. I am struck that just as Regina Coll quotes Francis of Assisi by saying, 'Let us go preach the gospel, using words if necessary,' this book is an opportunity to do just that: to preach the gospel in all forms that manifest the heart and soul of parish ministry."

Maria Harris
Writer and teacher

Regina Coll

The Heart and Soul of Parish Ministry

TWENTY-THIRD PUBLICATIONS

185 Willow Street • PO BOX 180 • MYSTIC, CT 06355
TEL: 1-800-321-0411 • FAX: 1-800-572-0788
E-MAIL: ttpubs@aol.com • www.twentythirdpublications.com

Twenty-Third Publications
A Division of Bayard
185 Willow Street
P.O. Box 180
Mystic, CT 06355
(860) 536-2611
(800) 321-0411
www.twentythirdpublications.com

ISBN:1-58595-182-X
Library of Congress Catalog Card Number: 00-2001135970
Printed in the U.S.A.

Contents

The Heart and Soul of Parish Ministry

Introduction

Have you ever wondered why people join a parish, why they return week after week to celebrate Eucharist, and why they turn to the parish in the glad and sad moments of their lives? When I asked some friends why each belonged to his or her parish, their answers ranged from, "I want to make sure my kids will be accepted in the school," to "It's our family tradition—my grandparents and parents came here," to "This parish has a reputation for being involved in social justice issues" (or for "good liturgy" or "excellent preaching"). As I pressed my friends to go beyond these somewhat superficial first responses, the conversations became similar. Each person, in his or her own way, was searching for help in living a better life, for meaning in their lives. They are all, in their own ways, searching for God.

Putting the question to ministers brings different yet quite similar answers. The first answer might be, "I am here to feed the hungry, or celebrate liturgy with the congregation, or preach the word as I understand it." If we ministers pursue our own answers far enough, we might answer, "We are here to make God's presence more apparent to people. We are here to help people recognize God in their lives."

At that point their answers begin to get at a fundamental truth of parish ministry: our primary purpose is not to conduct liturgies, to preach and teach, or to serve the poor and needy. These are only means to an end. We do those things so that we, and the people whom we serve, may come to a deeper relationship with God.

1

In order to prepare ministers for that extraordinary work, and in response to the overwhelming development of ministries in the past few decades, parishes and dioceses have established programs to train women and men for involvement in these ministries. Many dioceses have established competency standards for the various ministries, and they conduct workshops and conferences to implement that training. This book is meant to contribute to that process. It is meant for those in training for ministry, as well for all persons already engaged in parish work.

We begin in chapter one with some ideas about the connection between faith development and theological reflection. This is not a skills-building effort, or a chapter of how-to advice. (Polls and interviews with both clergy and laity reveal that the Catholic community is, for the most part, happy with the ministry provided by both ordained and lay ministers in their midst. Colleges, dioceses, and other institutions are doing yeoman's work in preparing so many so well in such a short time.) Rather, the theology I present here aims at establishing a firm faith foundation for ministry. Theological reflection enhances ministry even as ministry enhances theological reflection. Ministers bring a different lens to the endeavor than do professional theologians and are thus able to make different contributions. Theology complements ministry, guarding, as it does, against simple activism.

My aim is to suggest some of the foundational theological principles from which ministry develops. In chapter two, therefore, we will reflect on the various images of God that have sustained us through our lives. Our concept of God is basic to all ministry, indeed to all our relationships.

Multiplying metaphors for God allows us to plunge

deeper into the reality of a God who is with and for us. We are able to recognize something of God in the wide variety of human experiences, knowing that every human experience provides but a dim shadow of the divine life. And as we create a variety of metaphors for God, we understand that all metaphors limp; they both reveal and conceal. Each metaphor discloses some insight into who God is, but each metaphor also hides much about the Holy One.

Belief in a trinitarian God has so impressed itself on the Christian psyche that we imagine God as Three Someones or Three Somethings. We sometimes forget that Trinity, too, is a metaphor, not a definition of who God is. The dogma of the Trinity is a way for us to speak of God as relational. It provides a model for the way we are to relate to one another, and so it is valuable for ministers to ponder. Ministerial relationships at their best are trinitarian.

In chapter three we look at Jesus, God incarnate, who taught his first-century disciples, and us, the basics of ministry. We look to his life for inspiration and encouragement as we strive to minister. Jesus, of course, reveals who God is in unique and ultimate ways. It is not that we set Jesus up as an exact model to be imitated, as if we live and minister in ancient Palestine. Rather, we listen to his words and remember his deeds so that we may learn to minister to the needs of *this* time and place.

In chapter four, we consider how our beliefs about God, and our relationship with God, determine our beliefs about what it means to be human, what it means to be Christian. Belief in a loving, self-giving God establishes all of creation as good—including humanity. If, as a result, we have a positive view of humanity, we are not likely to be disposed to harsh judgments. We are not likely to focus attention on punishment, here or hereafter. Ministry will have a more compassionate face. I am not attempting to deny evil and sin but rather to place the spotlight on *grace*, God's gift of self. Indeed, focusing attention on God's self gift to us may be just the antidote to evil that we need in our world.

The final three chapters focus more directly on ministry. In chapter five we will discuss what it means to belong to a church that is so dramatically sacramental. The discussion of ministry necessarily follows that of church, because our mission and ministry flow from that of the church. In the last chapter we will focus on a spirituality for ministers.

CHAPTER ONE

Fostering Faith

The parish has only one job: fostering the relationship between God and parishioners. That, of course, involves fostering relationships among parishioners, and among parishioners and the rest of creation. Everything else—preaching, teaching, counseling, feeding the hungry, giving shelter to the homeless, celebrating the sacraments—is at the service of that one job. This one job, fostering relationships with God and God's creation, might be best thought of in terms of fostering faith. This is merely another way of saying that we are about the business of relating to God, of helping people to deepen that relationship, of enriching our own faith relationship with God.

For too long, many have thought of faith as a collection of truths, doctrines, rituals, and symbols that were called "the deposit of faith." Taking that idea of "deposit" seriously but also literally, it was deemed important to pass on to each succeeding generation a knowledge of the things that the church held dear. Older Catholics can remember homework that involved memorizing catechism answers along with spelling words, history dates, and multiplication tables. It was thought that committing church teachings to memory would insure the passing on of "the faith." And so we came to consider faith as a noun, a thing, rather than a vibrant action. But faith is something that we *do*; faith is a verb.

Faith Is a Verb

We speak of loving and hoping as human activities, as actions, as verbs, but we sometimes consider "faith" as something we own, something tangible, even static. Faith, however, is one of the ways we human beings know. To know by faith is different from knowing from experience or by science. It involves acceptance without proof, without personal experience; it involves acceptance based on the trustworthiness of those in whom we place our faith.

Faith has come to be considered a religious word, but, whether persons are religious or not, all human beings "faith" (remember, faith is a verb), just as all people love and hope. What is important here is to consider to what or to whom we commit our love, in what or in whom we hope, and in what or in whom we place our faith. For Christians, faith is acceptance and commitment to what has been revealed by God, especially in Jesus Christ.

But faith is more than simply knowing. It is not an intellectual endeavor. Faith is a way of relating to those in whom we faith. It is not a matter of *thinking* about God but rather a way of *relating* to God. It may be thought of in the same way as the biblical "to know"—intimately, physically, relationally. It is the foundation of our understanding of the Deity, our self-understanding, our understanding of the universe. That kind of relationship is nourished with prayer and service to one another. Christian faith, then, involves living a life of prayer and compassionate ministry.

For Christians, faith is founded on the teaching, life, death, and resurrection of Jesus Christ. Christians, following Paul (1 Cor 13:13), have linked faith, hope, and love, but have not always seen them as inseparable verbs connected so closely that it is difficult to discuss one without the others. Sharon Parks[1] speaks of loving tenderly as "the inherent vulnerability of 'faithing' persons." Walter Brueggemann maintains that "prophetic faith holds out the insistent hope that people like us can [bring about a transformation that is healing and joyous]."[2]

Adult Faithing

Because faith is a human activity, dynamic, lively, and active, it changes, waxes and wanes, develops and, when ignored, may dry up. Critical appropriation of faith, therefore, is the work of adult Christians, both individually and corporately. The church, as a whole, is strengthened by communities that struggle to better understand its teachings. Recent years have seen fits and starts toward this adult faith. In the words of Richard McBrien,

> Within Catholicism there has been a progressive movement, since Vatican II, away from a faith that is passive and childlike to one that is active and adult, and from a style that is controlling and paternalistic to a style that seeks to "rouse faith in [others] and to confirm them in faith, not to exert coercion upon them" (Declaration on Religious Freedom, n. 11).[3]

There is no such thing as real unquestioning faith; unthinking acceptance is not an adult response. Searching and questioning are the intelligent responses of faithful persons. Avery Dulles states it thus:

> To whip oneself up to an unfounded and merely subjective state of certitude is not faith but fanaticism. And to pretend to certitude that I do not possess is hypocrisy. . . Many people do not come to faith because they ask too few questions, not too many. When the mind is too full of its own certitudes it has no room for God.[4]

Careful reflection on the truths of our religious tradition may serve as a protection against literalizing the myths and stories that carry these truths. Superstition and fundamentalism may thus both be avoided. This careful reflection puts our faithing into an intimate partnership with religion and theology.

Faith and Religion

Faith and religion are often thought to be synonyms. They are not. Religion is an institution that is established to help express a group's faith. Religion helps people to live their faith; it provides myths, symbols, rites, and doctrines to support and foster faith. Christianity offers ways to foster faith in Jesus Christ and in the God who sent him.

Some have considered creeds, doctrines, and traditions to be the substance of faith. Important as these are, however, they are merely means to activating and fostering faith. They are meant to support our faith, to give us a shorthand means of expressing our faith, to get us started or to get us moving in our relationship with God. This is not to deny the importance of creeds, doctrines, and traditions in themselves, but rather to highlight their importance in fostering our relationship with God in faith. Even dogmas as esoteric as the Trinity and the Incarnation are meant to enable us to know, love, and worship God, to relate to God more intimately.

Faith and Theology

When we consciously reflect on our faith, think through what it is that we believe, and consider the consequences of our faith, we are in the realm of theology. So enamored have we been of the "simple faith" that sustained many holy ancestors that we have allowed a kind of anti-intellectualism to flourish concerning things theological. These times call for what McBrien, in the quote above, described as "active and adult" faith. That entails searching, questioning, and listening. It supposes knowing by heart.

We might get a better understanding of the relationship between faith and theology from the following analogy: theology is to faith as music criticism is to music. We study music criticism, not for itself, but to be able to better hear and appreciate music. Through our study, we are enabled to detect nuances not readily available to the uninitiated. We might say the same for theology. We do not study theology for itself, fascinating though it may be. We do theology to foster faith. Theology enables us to recognize nuances in our faith that may otherwise be lost to us. Theology is meant to enrich the faith life of the community.

St. Augustine challenged, "Believe that you may understand." That attempt to make faith intelligible is what St. Anselm referred to as "faith seeking understanding."

Theology is not an attempt to rationalize what is already held dear but to think about the consequences of faith in the life of the community. Theology's responsibility is not to find ways to defend what the magisterium proposes but to help people better understand and respond to church teaching. It is responsible for studying current expressions of church teaching to insure their fidelity to the gospel and tradition. Theology does not claim some kind of infused knowledge bestowed by God; it is hard work that demands integrity and fidelity.

Theologian Sallie McFague,[5] before she unpacks a theology that takes seriously not only the Christian tradition but also the challenging knowledge developed by modern science, warns us that "theology is often deceptively pretentious." Indeed, some theologians as well as some of the hierarchy do occasionally speak as if their ideas and concerns flow directly from the mind of God. When culture, sex, race, class, education, physical health, sexual orientation, and the like are forgotten, it may be difficult "to relativize contributions that sometimes masquerade under the cloak of objectivity, absoluteness or certainty." This is not meant to demean theologians or their work but merely to suggest that we maintain some prudence in accepting a particular theology too naively and without reflection.

Theology is contextual. Theologians of each age and clime use the wisdom and language of the people to articulate faith so that it may be more vibrant in the life of the community. The culture in which a theology develops has a significant effect on that theology. We are each so immersed in our own culture that it is difficult to recognize how cultural attitudes affect our thinking. And in each age the political, economic, and social tenor of the time affects the theology that develops. That theology either supports or challenges the prevailing wisdom of the day. Thomas Aquinas, attempting to make faith available to the people of his day, used the Aristotelean philosophy available in the thirteenth century to develop his theology. Today, theologians use the wisdom and knowledge available not only from philosophy, but also from science, social sciences, and the arts.

Theology Develops

Theology as a discipline is not finished. As long as God continues to act in our world, we are responsible for reflecting on and poring over God's ways so that we might recognize them and respond appropriately.

Liberation theologies have arisen in communities not previously heard from. Theologies that grow out of the experience of oppression or of racial prejudice allow for different metaphors, images, symbols, and myths than do theologies that spring from powerful and dominant cultures. They often provide new insights into the gospel message of Jesus Christ.

The idea that theologies, indeed doctrines, develop may be threatening for some, but church practices and teachings do change over time, as even a cursory look at history reveals. It took centuries and the influx of great numbers of Gentiles into the early church before the doctrines on Christ and the Trinity were developed. As these developing doctrines were promulgated, Christians needed to develop new thought patterns, new spiritualities, and new theologies that attempted to understand these critical teachings. In the eleventh century, when marriage was declared a sacrament, spouses and families formed new identities and relationships. Theologians helped by providing a strong foundation for the resulting changes in Christians' lives. Understanding marriage as a sign of God's presence makes that presence more available not only to the couple but to the whole community. It redefined the relationship between spouses and among the community. Attitudinal changes, however, take a long time. We are still struggling to learn what a truly sacramental marriage looks like.

In our own day, the documents produced by conferences of bishops and by theologians struggle with the images of church offered by Vatican II. Insights like Cardinal Bernardin's "seamless garment" and Pope John Paul II's "culture of death" are forcing us to take serious account of the just war theory and of the state's right to execute criminals, both of which have been strongly supported by the church in the past.

Cardinal John Henry Newman, in describing how doctrines develop, used the analogies of a child whose beliefs mature, of poetry that contains more than what was in the mind of the poet, and of the seed that grows into a bud and then a flower. In each case, the changes are rooted in original revelation and grow into something that may be a richer expression of the original—or at least an expression that may be more readily understood by subsequent generations. Vatican II says it thus:

> This tradition that comes from apostles develops in the church with the help of the Holy Spirit. For there is a growth in the understanding of realities and words which have been handed down. This happens through contemplation and studies made by believers, who treasure these

things in their hearts (cf. Luke 2:19, 51) through the intimate understanding of spiritual things they experience and
through preaching of those who have received through
episcopal succession the sure gift of truth. For as the centuries succeed one another, the church constantly moves
forward toward fullness of divine truth until words of God
reach their complete fulfillment in her. (*Dei Verbum*, 8)

How enriching for the life of the church that the bishops
at the Council spell out the contributions of all of us in this
endeavor. We believers contemplate and study, we treasure the tradition, we experience spiritual things, and we
trust the bishops to preach the truth. And so we all enable
the church to be and become what God wishes it to be.

Pastoral Theology

Lest anyone think that theologizing is the work and
responsibility of the experts and not of each Christian, let
us focus attention on that branch of theology labeled "pastoral." Pastoral theology makes the connection between
more classic and academic expressions of the church's
teaching and the life of the Christian community. It is the
theology that asks "so what?" after contemplation of the
profound truths of our religion. What should a community that professes belief in the Incarnation look like? What
effect does Eucharist have on the life of a Christian? How
does faith in the dogma of the Trinity affect our relationships?

Pastoral theology is that theology that focuses on the
church's efforts to continue the mission of Christ in the
church and the world. To think about the mission of the
church and ministry is to engage in the process of learning
and developing a pastoral theology. Reflecting on ministry

raises questions such as: why do we visit the sick, feed the hungry, console the grieving? Why do we teach Scripture to children, preach the gospel, share Eucharist? The answers we come to probably lead to even deeper and more profound questions. This ongoing reflection enriches our faith, deepens it, and makes it possible for us to articulate it so that others may also deepen their faith.

Let me repeat: all ministry is about fostering faith in the people of God. We minister to deepen the faith life of the whole community, not just to alleviate the suffering of a few, terrible as that suffering may be. All ministry is about the coming of the reign of God, that community to which Jesus called all his disciples. It follows, then, as I have already insisted, that the parish has only one reason for being—to foster faith among the community. Everything else—preaching, teaching, counseling, feeding the hungry, giving shelter to the homeless, celebrating the sacraments—is at the service of fostering faith.

Ministry—A Faithful Response

The challenge to really live out our faith is the critical issue for all Christians but especially for those who have been called to leadership in the community as ministers. It was what St. Francis was trying to tell his brothers when he said, "Let us go preach the gospel, using words if necessary." In the same way, an ancient rabbi challenged those who spent their lives studying the Torah. He insisted that they did not have to teach and preach the Torah if they lived in such a way that people could read the Torah in their very lives.

Ministry is rooted in the faith life of the minister and of

the community. Christians minister in response to the teachings of Jesus, who told parables, healed sick people, and shared table with persons who were reviled by society. He called on his followers to do likewise. Disciples of an earlier era and disciples today accept the challenge because of their faith in Jesus Christ.

To have faith in Christ means that we place our hope in the promise of resurrection and that we strive to love God with our whole heart and our neighbor as ourselves. Neither that hope nor that love are possible without faith.

Pastoral ministry has been described as the care of souls; but "care of souls" demands care of bodies. It is how the church nourishes faith, how it enables Christians to enflesh the doctrines, rituals, metaphors, and symbols that define our faith in Christ. So how does our faithing lead to ministry?

Getting Ideals and Actions in Synch

Paul said it best. "I cannot understand my own actions. I do not do what I want to do but what I hate " (Rom 7:15). Like Paul, our ideals and behaviors often do not match. Theologically, we would say that our professed theology outstrips our operative theology. What we profess to believe, what we state as our deepest ideals are not always strong enough to overcome the weakness in our being that Paul talks about.

It may be helpful to write a list of "I believe" statements. That list indicates our professed theology, but a theology that is not incarnated is no theology at all. A theology that is not evident from our lives is no theology at all. This incarnation of our professed theology is our operative theology.

Unless we attend to our professed theology, it is difficult to measure our operative theology by those basic beliefs. The point, of course, is to be able to tell one from the other. Lifestyle and how we treat others reveal much about our professed theology. The way we use our time, energy, talents, possessions, what we choose to keep around us, how we decorate our space, how we live out who we are, also tell us what our operative theology is about. More important, they tell us how deeply we hold to what we profess.

Get It in Writing

The daily demands of ministry can be so overwhelming that little time or energy is left for checking in to our basic and fundamental motivations and beliefs about why we minister. I would suggest that setting these in writing and keeping them available may help determine the nature of our ministry. It may even help to keep us on track and not get lost in the fray. Individual ministers and ministerial teams may benefit from putting their theology of ministry in writing, that is, putting in writing what it is we pledge ourselves to be and do when we undertake to minister to the people of God.

Luke records some advice Jesus gave to the disciples: "If one of you were going to build a tower, wouldn't you first sit down and calculate the outlay to see if you have enough money to complete the project?" (Luke 14:28). He was suggesting that they don't jump into things they are not ready for. When we plan a trip, many of us go to AAA, get maps, study them, and keep referring to them as we travel along. The Boy Scouts say "be prepared." It is their equivalent of the slogan you see in some businesses: "Think ahea..." where the last letter doesn't quite fit on the plaque.

As we enter upon ministry, it is well for us to take Jesus' words to heart. Sitting down and calculating the cost, mapping out the trip, being prepared, and thinking ahead are all ways of knowing where we are going, of keeping us from losing our way.

In the past thirty years mission statements have become all the rage. Parishes and dioceses as well as large and small corporations, government offices, universities, and kindergartens are all writing mission statements. That is a really good first step toward getting the job done—whatever the job is that needs to be done. But often the big problem is that once groups have gone to the trouble of writing a mission statement, they put it away somewhere safe so it will not be lost. They do not keep it alive. They are like the servant in Matthew's gospel, who, receiving only one talent, buried it so as not to lose it (Mt 25:14–30).

Don't Forget!

Mission statements should be a lively, pulsing presence in every facet of life, like the Shema, treasured by generation after generation of Jews. "Hear, O Israel! The Lord is our God alone! Therefore you shall love the Lord, your God will all your heart and with all your soul and with all your strength." Recorded right after the account of the giving of the Ten Commandments to Moses, the Scripture gives the first great commandment that Jesus, good Jew that he was, could recite by heart when he had to.

But giving the foundational command is not enough—it could be forgotten. The Bible commands, "Take to heart the words which I enjoin on you today. Drill them into your children. Speak of them at home and abroad, whether you are busy or at rest. Bind them on your wrist as a sign and let them be as a pendant on your forehead. Write them on the doorposts of your houses and your gates" (Deut 6:6–9). To this day, Orthodox Jews wear the tefilin containing the sacred words. We know them as phylacteries from the warning in Matthew's gospel not to imitate those who wore the phylacteries in such a manner as to show off their supposed piety. The warning is that our inner thoughts and motivation ought to be in synch with what we present to others.

Devout Jews are reminded to reverence the Shema every time they enter or leave the house. Even many Jews who describe themselves as non-observant post a mezuzah (a case containing the holy words) on their doorposts and reverently kiss it as they enter or leave. It may be the way of reminding themselves that however loose their formal connection with Judaism, they are still Jews and cling to the foundation of Judaism—loving God with their whole heart, soul, and spirit.

Even though I am not Jewish, I have set a mezuzah on the doorpost of my home as a reminder of that first great commandment we share with our Jewish brothers and sisters. I touch it with awe and respect for what it has meant over the ages and for what it means in people's lives, including my own, today.

The Shema seems to be saying, "Don't forget! Don't forget! Don't forget!" And the way not to forget is to surround ourselves with reminders—teach your children; talk about it; keep it on your person; decorate your house with it.

That's the model for what to do with parish mission statements. I am not suggesting that we wear them on our foreheads or attached to our wristwatches, but simply that we have to devise ways to be ever mindful of what we have been sent by God to do and what we have promised to deliver.

A good way for a parish to keep a mission statement alive is to print it in bulletins, newsletters, and appeal letters. Announce it from the rooftops. Say to everyone, especially one another, "This is why we are called; this is what we are trying to do, this is who we are and who we hope to become." That public announcement gives us a little more impetus to actually be and do what, in our best moments, we pledge ourselves to be and to do. On the other hand, raising expectations by announcing a mission statement and not living up to it disappoints people and may lead to loss of trust and hope.

Another way of keeping a mission statement alive is to read it before every staff or team meeting and every meeting of the parish council. Refer to it when major decisions are in the balance. Ask what decision is suggested in the light of that statement. That may help us to avoid making decisions in response to particular needs without asking if it fits in with what we believe we have been called to and what we have promised.

I once worked for almost a year with a group writing a mission statement. One of the main pieces of this document described how they would work together. After long and intense discussions they pledged to work together in a collaborative way. The job done, they filed their mission statement away with other important papers. When, a few months later, the director of the group hired a new staff member without consultation, he could not understand why the other members of the group were upset. Each had a different understanding of what "collaborative" meant.

They had not kept the document alive. They had not measured their operative theology by their professed one.

Sometimes, difficult paths will be chosen because we keep in mind our best ideals, and, sometimes, very good programs and projects may be decided against because they do not fit in with how we understand ourselves to be called by God. Fidelity to mission as understood and articulated in a mission statement reminds us that we cannot do everything but that we can be faithful to what we have been called to do.

This is not to suggest that the mission statement is a way of getting out of responding to needs. It is, rather, to take seriously a caution from Thomas Merton: "To allow oneself to be carried away by a multitude of conflicting concerns, to surrender to too many demands, to commit oneself to too many projects, to want to help everyone in everything is to succumb to violence." The mission statement is meant to focus our energies to care for that portion of God's good earth that has been given us. We cannot do everything, but a mission statement may help us to do well what we have committed ourselves to do. Mission statements are not blueprints or syllabi; they are not carved in stone. They are statements of our best ideals and dreams that may be used as the foundation for concrete plans and programs.

Developmental Theory of Faith Development

I have already suggested that questioning and investigating matters of doctrine and belief are important, even necessary, facets of adult faith. Faith changes and grows—and, unfortunately, it sometimes dies. Patterns of faith development have been suggested by James Fowler and have been used by generations of catechists and religious educators.

Fowler devised a scheme describing the journey from the fantasy-based faith of a child through stages of literal interpretation, and peer-influenced faith, to more personal experiences of faith. His last two stages of faith describe, first, the ability to recognize truth in positions other than the one we hold and, finally, the ability of a person to live out the two great commandments of which Jesus spoke: love of God and love of neighbor as oneself. Very few people attain this final stage; among them we might list Mahatma Gandhi, St. Francis of Assisi, and, of course, Jesus.

I have resisted the temptation to spell out in greater detail this developmental scheme because of the simplistic and dangerous uses to which it has sometimes been put. There is a danger of concretizing each stage and pigeonholing people at one level or another, and that would be disastrous to ministry. The theory may be helpful, however, in preparing programs, lectures, homilies, and in counseling. In order to facilitate growth in faith, it is first necessary for ministers to understand how people faith at different points in their lives.

The Only Work of the Parish

This chapter began with the bold statement that the parish has only one job. No matter how busy we are with the myriad ways of ministering, our only real job is to enable those we serve to intensify and strengthen their relationship with God. In the light of our reflections on faith, I would suggest that together parish ministers measure and weigh programs, liturgies, preaching, and teaching to insure that they are at the service of faith. Helping parishioners deepen their relationship with God, with others, and with all of creation is the exalted work to which we have been called. In the process our own relationship with God will flourish.

SUMMARY

1. The parish has only one job: fostering and enriching the relationship between God and people. Everything we do should contribute to that relationship.

2. The creeds, doctrines, and traditions of our religion are expressions of our faith and means for fostering and deepening that faith.

3. Theology is the servant of faith. It is meant to enable us to better incarnate our faith. It is the work of the parish minister to assist people to better articulate their faith (professed theology) and, more important, to live according to that profession (operative theology). Concrete reminders, including such things as mission statements, help in keeping professed theology and operative theology congruent.

4. Theology affects and is affected by the culture in which it develops. The wide range of theologies that have developed over the ages give witness to the wide range of different experiences of God among different peoples.

5. As persons mature, faith matures and raises new questions. Developing an adult faith involves the

ongoing struggle of searching for answers. Parish ministers have no greater responsibility than helping in this search.

POINTS FOR REFLECTION

Avery Dulles maintains that some people never come to an adult appropriation of faith because they ask too few questions. How can a parish team help parishioners struggle with their questions so that their faith may be deepened rather than threatened?

Learn something of a theology from a community other than your own (black, feminist, latino/a, traditional, etc.). What challenges or affirmations does that theology provide for your own?

What effect does Pope John Paul II's criticism of "the culture of death" and Cardinal Bernardin's ethic of "the seamless garment" have on parish programs? preaching? teaching?

Make a short list of "I believe" statements. Then, next to each, write, "therefore I..." Notice how your professed theology and operative theology are related.

Write or discover a prayer to be said before you read, study, or reflect. Make it part of your daily routine.

CHAPTER TWO

Imaging God

What image of God comforted or challenged you when you were a child? What images of God no longer suffice? Perhaps God was like the *Deus ex machina* in an ancient Greek or Roman drama, who came in on pulleys when things got tough. Or perhaps God was like the scary image of Santa keeping a book on everything we did wrong. Somehow, in spite of the longstanding belief that God is Love, we have passed on unworthy images and metaphors about God from generation to generation.

God of the Jews

The genius of the Israelites, who were able to perceive God in the sufferings and joys of the people, was to introduce a God who did not live and make love or war with other gods in another sphere. The Israelites came to appreciate the one God, who chose to be involved in the history of the people. God intervened on behalf of the Israelites, made covenants with them, and was faithful to those covenants. God was involved in history. The God of Abraham and Sarah was not indifferent to the needs of the people.

God's Revelation in Christ

The life, death, and resurrection of Jesus unveil even greater insights into God. God was not content simply to be involved in the life of Israel. God elected to come and live among us, to be one of us. Jesus, truly and fully human, enables us to understand more deeply who God is. Jesus, truly and fully God, enables us to relate to God more intimately. Transcendence and immanence come together, without diminishing or destroying one another.

Belief in the divinity of Jesus eradicates concepts of God as remote and immutable. God has become one of us; God knows from experience what it means to be human. We know from that human being what God is like. Jesus' compassion for poor and oppressed people, his healing sick and diseased persons, his sharing meals with all sorts of people, his self-giving love all provide penetrating insights into divinity.

God's Revelation in Our Day

We can trust that our experience of God is who God is. God does not reveal falsities about the divine life. God has chosen to provide clues, to give hints, to draw traces of divinity in human experience—the experience of all human beings.

It is well for all of us, then, to be open to learn from persons with different experiences of God, to take into consideration images and metaphors for God that are not part of our own cultural background. Black, Hispanic, and European theologies challenge, color, and enrich one another. Feminist, Womanist, and Mujerista theologies add to the mix. More recently, the challenges from the scientific community attach even greater intensity and richness. Ministry that takes seriously these contributions will itself take on greater radiance. Our reflection and contemplation of the myriad ways God reveals Godself in our world helps to open us to greater wisdom into whom it is we know as Love.

It may be easy to find God in the magnificence of nature, in brilliant sunsets, majestic mountain peaks, roaring ocean waves. It may also be easy to find God in the intensely human experiences of birth and death. But God is not present only in poetic and profound moments. God is always with us. Recognizing God in the monotonous, ordinary events of life enables us to say that every moment is holy, all life sacred. Recognizing God, however, does not mean that life will be easy and cozy. As Joyce Rupp challenges,

> No matter how intentional and mindful we are of God's presence, we are living in disillusionment and setting ourselves up for failure if we expect everyday at work to be a felt, mystical deep union experience with God.[1]

Ministering toward the Reign of God

As I stressed in chapter one, we do not give the cup of water simply to relieve thirst; we do not provide housing simply to shelter from the cold and rain; we do not visit the sick and bury the dead simply to comfort and console individuals. Wonderful as these works are in themselves, as ministers we are committed to these works in order to help firmly establish the coming reign of God among us. That simply means the coming of God among us; or better—the recognition of God who is already present among us. Feeding the hungry, clothing the naked, caring for the poor, bringing about reconciliation, and preaching the gospel are works that make God's presence among us more evident.

What a profound responsibility is ours! The only thing we have to do is to do *whatever* we do so that people will be able to come to know and love God. And so our conversation about faith must begin with a reflection on how we image God and how we ourselves understand God's action with and for us.

Imaging God

It is certainly true that our image of God and our self image are closely related. Because of this symmetry, our image of God is closely related to how we minister. People can read our theology in our actions. Because God is the fundamental and ultimate focus of our faith, let us take time to review how we may understand this relationship with God.

The Hebrew Scriptures give strong warning about how we are to relate to God. The first two commandments given to Moses are warnings we need to heed in our own day if we are to live faithfully. The commandment to avoid false gods is not addressed only to pagans and polytheists. Not taking the Lord's name in vain is not just a condemnation for perjurers and people who curse others. The prohibition against strange gods has often been spiritualized and allegorized to mean that we shouldn't make money or success or fame or our own wants into gods. (Given the perks of church employment, ministers are not so likely to be guilty of that.)

What strange gods might we have kept hidden in our hearts? Are our ideas and concepts about God so small, so restricted, so puny that they better describe an ogre than God? We might ask if our images of God are themselves idols of a sort, if we have, in effect, imaged God in a way unworthy of divinity. I sometimes think that we may have to apologize to God when we finally meet face-to-Face. God may ask us, "What is this you've been saying of Me?"

Strange Gods

All images of God are inadequate; nothing that we humans can construct remotely approaches who God is. Theologians tell us that God is ineffable, unutterable, inde-scribable, unspeakable, beyond words. Then they write thousand-page tomes talking about the divine mystery. That's just it—saying God is ineffable means that we must constantly struggle to find ways that are less inadequate than others for speaking about the Holy One. None of our images of God is great enough to capture the divine essence, and yet we must keep searching for ways to help one another overcome our misunderstandings of who God is. We must continue to reflect on our images of God that may hide, or even distort, more than they reveal.

Among the most destructive images of God is the one suggesting that God demands or wills sufferings and pain, and that blames God for human suffering. If we tell people that a loved one's death is all for the best or that poverty and hunger are somehow God's will, how can they believe in such a God? How can they love such a God? In our ministry to people who are suffering, let us be careful not to impugn God or to suggest that pain and sorrow are tests that God puts us through to see if we are worthy.

Some responses to major tragedies, sympathetic as they are meant to be to the suffering of those who lost family and friends, evoke this God image. Mourning the loss of the infants and young children who have died, some leave signs that say, "God needs more angels in heaven" and "God's will is not ours." Sometimes grief is so overwhelming that people resort to what they think are comforting words without thinking what they really mean. Silence may be the more appropriate response.

Another image of God that ministers need to be careful about presenting is the God of the gap, the God whom we call on when we have done everything, but nothing has worked. This is the God who seems to be pushed to the margins by modern technology and science. People used to bless the house with holy water during fearsome storms; now we erect lightning rods. People used to have great processions to avert a plague; now we inoculate against all sorts of diseases. People used to pray for protection for crops; now we fertilize and irrigate the fields. But when all efforts fail, then we turn to God. After running from doctor to doctor, we find ourselves on our knees begging for a cure. This God has been pushed to the margins and is called in only in emergencies that we are powerless to control ourselves. We forget God's involvement in the technological and scientific advancements and act as if we have grown beyond the need for God's involvement in our lives. The lightning rods, inoculations, irrigation, and fertilization methods are God's gifts. Medical advances are God's gifts.

And what about the image of the God who weighs and measures everything in this life so as to reward or punish in the next? This is another inadequate God. This is the God who keeps account of every fault, failing, and sin. It is an image of a God who created this life as just a trial period for the next. When God gazed on creation and said, "It is good" the message was not, "It is a good testing ground."

Fear of punishment and desire for reward are low level modes of moral thinking and unworthy of the people of God. This image of a harsh and unforgiving God has turned many people away from the God of whom Jesus spoke.

All of this is not to suggest that we speak of God in sentimental and maudlin terms. We can turn to the sacred Scriptures to discover a host of strong images: rock, fire, water, roaring lion, hovering mother bird, potter, judge, baker woman, artist, liberator, companion, friend, lover, father, mother—to name but a few. We can turn to the images of God that Jesus gave: a good shepherd who goes in search of a sheep that was lost, a woman who sweeps the house in search of a lost coin, and a parent who runs out to meet the prodigal child; and also the owner of an estate who pays everyone the same, no matter how long each has labored.

Each image tells us something, but even taking all the names and images together does not begin to hint at who God is. Trying to capture who God is may be a bit like trying to describe how you love someone. You might recount their virtues, describe incidents that give insight into their character and personality, tell of the wonder of their beauty, and finally have to say, "Yes, but, that's really not it." Still, it is necessary to try.

Relational God

Jewish people at Passover sing a litany in which the response is Dayenu—it would have been enough. They repeat, "If God had only done thus and so and not also...Dayenu. It would have been enough." We Christians can sing a similar litany.

If God had only revealed divinity to us in the wonders of creation and not in overwhelming love and concern for the Israelites,
    Dayenu—it would have been enough.

If God had only shown overwhelming love and concern for the Israelites and not become one of us in the incarnation,
    Dayenu—it would have been enough.

If God had only become one of us in the incarnation and not promised that the Spirit would be with us always,
    Dayenu—it would have been enough.

But this God who created us, who entered history in the lives of the Israelites, who became one of us, and who remains with us, has also loved each of us into being and promises to live with us forever. It would have been enough, it would have been enough, it would have been enough. How much more must God do before we are convinced that God is indeed Love?

The God whom we worship is not a remote being sitting in solitary grandeur. Our God is personal, relational, communal; that is what we are trying to say in the doctrine of the Trinity. Catherine LaCugna says: "The doctrine of the Trinity affirms that the 'essence' of God is relational, otherward, that God exists as diverse persons united in a communion of freedom, love and knowledge."[2]

The God whom we worship is trinitarian, although not many of us consider that enough. Oh yes, in the name of the Trinity, we baptize; in the name of the Trinity, we celebrate Eucharist; in the name of the Trinity, we bless ourselves. (Hear what has just been said—*we bless ourselves.* Each of us has the power and responsibility not only to bless others in celebrating baptism and Eucharist with them; more astonishingly, we have the power, the right, and the responsibility to bring God's blessings upon ourselves. It is a wonderfully exciting thought.)

Much as we sign ourselves in the name of the Trinity, however, we do not often carry over the belief in the Trinity to our daily life. In fact, Karl Rahner suggested that if the church officially announced a change in trinitarian theology, it would have little impact on the Christian community. In other words, if tomorrow morning's newspapers reported that the Vatican had declared that there is a fourth person, making the Trinity a Quaternity, there would be no great reaction from Christians. Certainly there would not be a reaction like there was to *Humanae Vitae* in 1968. That is because the doctrine of the Trinity does not serve as a foundation in most Christians' lives.

The doctrine of the Trinity is an affirmation that our experience of God gives us clues about who God is—true-enough clues so that we can have confidence that God is constantly revealing who God is. The God who is recognized in the awesome goodness of creation, who sided with the Israelites, who is incarnate in Jesus, and who is manifest in the ongoing presence of the Spirit among us—this is who God is. Our experience of God can be trusted. God is not other than what is revealed to us. Catherine LaCugna says that

The very nature of God who is self-communicating love is expressed in what God does in the events of redemptive history. There is no hidden God (deus absoconditus) behind the God of revelation history, no possibility that God is in God's eternal mystery other than what God reveals Godself to be.[3]

When we say that God is trinitarian we are really saying that, in God's very being, God is communal. Sara Maitland suggests a charming symbol that may illustrate—better than St. Patrick's shamrock—the inner dependence and mutuality of the Trinity. She says, "My favorite model of the Trinity is that it is like a child's pigtail."[4] If one strand of the braid is pulled out, there is no more braid at all but if one petal of the shamrock is pulled off, the other two petals are still somewhat related. The pigtail is an image that suggests that a God who is not trinitarian, communal, relational, is not God.

God's being, as we know it from experience, is communal, mutual, related. Our understanding of the Trinity provides that model for the way we are to live and be with one another. The dogma of the Trinity, according to Elizabeth Johnson, is a shorthand attempt to describe how we humans have experienced God.

Far from being literally descriptive, the trinitarian symbol desires to express and protect the fundamental Christian experience of shalom drawing near. It is shorthand for the dynamic, inexpressible Sophia-God of compassionate, liberating love who is involved in history in multifaceted ways... It is a pointer to holy mystery in trust that God really is the compassionate, liberating God encountered through Jesus in the Spirit.[5]

If we are to be perfect as God is perfect (Mt 5:48), then the dogma of the Trinity provides guidelines for Christian life. "God's very nature is to exist toward and for another…. Entering into divine life therefore is impossible unless we also enter into a life of love and communion with others."[6] The doctrine exists not only to provide theologians something to ponder and debate about. It is a doctrine, like all doctrines, to be lived. The Trinity provides a model for families, for communities, for the church, for all relationships.

The church, in all its manifestations, is the sacrament of the Trinity, the icon, if you will, of God. When we as church foster community, when we enable relationships of mutuality, when we uphold the dignity of all the people of God, we are sacraments of the Trinity. In healing broken bodies, in confronting systematic evil, in repairing fractured relationships, the church is making visible to all the God in whom we trust. The church exists to bring God's grace, that is, God's very life, to the world. It is not that grace itself but an icon, a sacrament of that divine life.

The famous fifteenth-century icon of the Trinity by Andrei Rublev, depicting the three angels who visited Abraham and Sarah, strikingly illustrates what is expected of us. The table of hospitality and welcome shared by the three visitors is open and draws the viewer in.

Classical artists like Rublev are not the only ones who provide profound images of God. A young volunteer missionary who had just returned from Chile shared her image of God with a group of us when she invited us into the space where she found God. "If God is love," she said while holding up a picture, "then this is what God is like." The picture was of Mary and Elizabeth hugging each other when they met at what we have come to call the visitation. As she described the love and support shared by the women among whom she had ministered, we entered into her experience of God.

The relationality of which I speak does not suppose that God is the great partner who does not need us but that God has entered into community with us and, in that sense, needs us. The Eucharist is a marvelous symbol of what I mean. God provides grain[7] from the bounty of the earth. But they were only sheaves of wheat or barley or perhaps some grain not available to us today; good for nibbling on until some genius forbear of ours crushed the kernels into flour and formed them into masses, heated them up on hot stones or under ashes of a dying fire, and created something wonderful—bread. So wonderful that Solomon is said to have paid for the cedars and cypress needed for the construction of the Temple with twenty thousand measures of wheat.

In the same way, God provided vines heavy with delicious grapes. One day, another genius ancestor stomped on grapes and left the juice lying around for a while until it became an intoxicating drink. Again, God's wonderful gifts were transformed into something wonderfully different.

The gifts of God were taken by human beings and transformed into something quite other. At every Eucharist, we pray "Fruit of the vine and work of human hands." Together, God's gift and human effort are necessary for the celebration of Eucharist. In the same way, God's gift and human effort are necessary for the coming of the reign of God.

It is a truism that the church is most profoundly church when celebrating Eucharist. Eucharist is not just the hour or so we spend together in church on Sunday. We bring the church, the whole world, and particular needs of suffering persons to prayer. At the presentation of the gifts we carry not only the bread and wine but the lives of all the congregation. In the closing minutes, we are enjoined to continue the Eucharist, going in peace to love and serve the Lord. Eucharist involves all of creation. We might then, take Eucharist as a model for ministry in much the same way that Joanmarie Smith models teaching:

> In a world where the incarnation reinforces our conviction that God is thoroughly present, that this is a universe drenched with divinity, the Blessed Sacrament is not an exception to the rest of reality but a clue to it. And grateful worship/adoration is the most appropriate response. Moreover, since the primordial expression of that response is the Great Thanksgiving, it behooves us to shape our [ministry] into a form of Eucharist.[8]

SUMMARY

1. God, as revealed to the Jews, is a God who is involved in the history and life of the people.

2. In the life, death, and resurrection of Jesus, God is revealed more intimately.

3. God the Holy Spirit continues to reveal Godself to us and will continue to guide the church, according to the promise of Jesus.

4. Ministry in all its forms is concerned with bringing about the reign of God. Everything that ministers do is aimed at making God more present in the lives of people.

5. False images of God, such as the God who wills or

allows evil for our good, the God of the gaps, and the God who gives us human life as a test or trial are all unworthy of God who is Love.

6. The dogma of the Trinity affirms that God is relational and exists in a communion of Love.

7. Belief in the Trinity provides us with a foundation for how we are to live our lives as individual Christians and as church.

Points for Reflection

What childhood images of God have you outgrown? Is there anything that challenges your current images of God?

How does faith in the dogma of the Trinity affect your personal relationships? How does it affect the life of your parish?

What popular images of God may be unworthy of a God who loves us unconditionally?

What do the liturgies, educational programs, and outreach programs of your parish reveal of God?

What points may be important to include in a discussion with adults about God?

CHAPTER THREE

Coming to Know Christ

Some Christians seem to hold that Jesus' humanity was only a mask hiding his divinity. Because Jesus was divine, they might suggest, Jesus knew all things, past, present, and future. This leaves no room for growth in wisdom or knowledge, no room for surprise in his life. He is pictured in gleaming white garments, untouched by the dusty roads, as if he floated a few inches above the dirt. He is never imaged as tired, dirty, worn out, or haggard. Even more, he is imaged as untouched by the people who filled his life. Not much is made of the impact his parents had on his sensitivity to others or his fidelity to his God. We can only conjecture how the twelve-year-old boy who amazed the teachers in the Temple acquired his wisdom.

In fact, preaching ordinarily and appropriately focuses on the impact of Jesus on those around him. But hardly a word is ever said about the influence those people had on *him*. In a class with undergraduates, I shared some contemporary insights on the person of Mary Magdalene—such as the lack of scriptural support for identifying her as a prostitute, her fidelity in following Jesus during his lifetime, and her being the first person to whom Jesus chose to appear after his resurrection. I closed the lecture with, "Imagine what it was like for her to be loved by Jesus," to which a student replied, "Imagine what it was like for Jesus to be loved by such a woman." Imagine, indeed.

Shifting the spotlight to the humanity of Jesus is not to be understood as a denial of his divinity. Jesus is, as we confess each Sunday, "God from God, Light from Light, true God from true God." His humanity is not in conflict with his divinity. In Jesus, God's self-giving fills the human longing for the infinite. "God who is always self-expressing within the divine nature now self-expresses outside the divine nature, in time, in human nature, in another medium (you might say) and the one who comes into existence is Jesus of Nazareth, the Word made flesh."[1]

Jesus is not half god, half human but all God, all human. This mystery was not recognized until after his resurrection. Then his followers perceived something new about God, whom they had seen in human form. They could better understand who God is because they had seen who Jesus is. And so they began to speak of Jesus of Nazareth as Jesus Christ, the anointed one of God.

Jesus the Jew

Jesus lived and died a Jew. He was born of a Jewish mother and grew up in a Jewish home. His friends were Jews. His holy days and customs were Jewish. He lived as a Jew under Roman occupation and longed for the release of

Israel from oppression. The prayers he prayed were Jewish. Jesus knew the Jewish Scriptures well enough to understand his own life in their light. Even his last words were a Jewish lament from Psalm 22, "My God, my God, why have you forsaken me?"

Judaism had a profound effect on the early church. Its Scriptures were not only accepted as the "old" part of the church's own but they also informed much of what is written in the new. Every Eucharist recalls the celebration of the Passover feast. We can only imagine what history would look like if Christians remembered through the centuries that Jesus was born of a Jewish mother, and lived and died a Jew. In his Jewishness, he related in a unique way to the God of Abraham and Sarah and taught about the one God whom Judaism had introduced to the world.

The Gospels

Reverence for the word of God has been carried to the point of imagining that God dictated the gospels to a secretary-evangelist who merely transferred the words to a scroll without contributing to them at all. It is as if some kind of "automatic writing" were involved, where the writer is no more than an instrument, like a pen, a typewriter, or a computer. When we speak of the gospels as the revealed word of God, we are not suggesting that God sent an angel to whisper in the ear of the evangelist. That is not how God works with us. God works through human agency, as our own history as well as the history of the Hebrews and the early Christians teach so well.

Revelation is the ongoing process whereby the Spirit of God continues to disclose God's gift of Self to us. The

Spirit aroused the memories of Jesus' disciples, cultivated faith in the persons who listened to the disciples speak of their memories, and inspired some persons to seek to preserve that faith in written form. Revelation continued as the early church preserved and accepted some of these writings as its canon, its official Scripture. (This is not to suggest that other works, called apocrypha, may not serve as revelation but that they are not part of the list or canon that serves as the criterion for the church in its teaching concerning Jesus.)

In the days after the resurrection, disciples of Jesus preached his message to the people they encountered in the environs of Jerusalem and on missionary journeys. They passed on memories of Jesus, repeated parables they had heard, described healings and conversions, and shared the painful remembrance of his last days, all in the light of the resurrection. There was no need for a written account, believing, as they did, that Jesus would return very soon.

As eyewitnesses died off, the stories needed to be preserved in some formal way to insure that the memories would be preserved. And so, the evangelists penned the gospels, each for his own community, hardly imagining that persons from another time and place would read them for inspiration. The written accounts grew out of the oral tradition that each community held dear. What we read, then, is what the early followers of Jesus lifted up for the deepening of their own faith. At each step in the development of the gospels, God spoke to and in the Christian community.

The memories of Jesus' teaching and ministry are filtered through the lens of the resurrection—when Jesus of

Nazareth was recognized by his disciples as Jesus Christ, God's anointed one. These gospels are faith statements, meant to help the community grow in faith. They are not historical documents, much less biographies. They did not record any of Jesus' physical features, his height, coloring, or mannerisms. Apparently, the evangelists had little interest in giving us a word picture of Jesus.

The Ministry of Jesus

At the beginning of his public life, Jesus announced his mission. Adapting Isaiah, he stood in the synagogue and proclaimed:

> The spirit of God has been given to me, for God has anointed me.
> God has sent me to bring good news to the poor;
> to proclaim liberty to captives; and to the blind, new sight,
> to set the downtrodden free and to proclaim God's year of favor. (Luke 4:17–19)

During his ministry, Jesus lived what he had proclaimed. He healed people of all kinds of infirmities, freed people from what enslaved them, and announced the Good News to the poor. As Kenan Osborne has said, through Jesus, "Men and women are restored to wholeness. His ministry to the outcasts is boundary-breaking, stepping across the religiously and socially accepted division of clean and unclean."[2] Jesus touched the unclean leper; he was touched by the hemorrhaging woman; he healed on the Sabbath. Always putting the needs of people before the Law (much as he respected the Law), he shattered the boundaries that divided people. Jesus, filled with the Spirit of God, established relationships and repaired community by eliminating barriers between people, thus giving an example in his life of the inclusive reign of God that he preached.

Through the ages many characteristics of Jesus' ministry have been offered for our edification and inspiration. Here, I offer just three suggestions: The ministry of Jesus was incarnate, prophetic, and empowering.

Incarnate

The dictionary uses words like fleshly, bodily, material, and human to define incarnate. Ministry takes these things seriously. It answers the bodily, material, and human needs of people. It is involved with flesh, as a look at the ministry of Jesus illustrates. Jesus used things of the earth: dirt, spit, wine, bread. He touched people and was touched. His service was not antiseptic, clean. Jesus was comfortable with the things of earth. All the stories he told spoke of the stuff of the earth.

We cannot minister in the abstract. Ministry is not antiseptic or clean. It often involves being enmeshed in differences, disagreements, and disillusionments. Ministry involves touching broken hearts and battered bodies. Entering into the suffering of others does not leave us untouched. It means getting our hands dirty, both literally and figuratively, and sometimes it means our hearts will be broken. The ministry of Jesus suggests that the reign of God, to which he was so profoundly committed, breaks into our world whenever bodies and souls are healed, relationships are restored, and justice and peace are established.

Jesus described heaven as a banquet full of good things to eat and drink and good companionship to share that feast. Ministry also involves preparing feasts that give a taste of the heavenly banquet. That may mean feeding the many hungers from which people suffer or celebrating the numerous joyous occasions of people's lives. Of course, it finds its fullest meaning in our celebration of Eucharist.

"Carne," the root of our word incarnation, means flesh. An incarnational approach to ministry (and to all of Christian life) suggests that we may need a theology of sexuality that celebrates this wondrous gift. We seem to be a people who are out of touch with our senses. Many are not able to name parts of their own bodies. We speak of sex as "dirty." No wonder "save it for the one you will marry" makes so little sense to young and not-so-young people. A theology of sexuality is developing that takes seriously the relational nature of human beings. We are made from the relationship of our parents and grow in the community of family and friends. We become fully human and Christian in relationships. Catherine LaCugna reminds us,

> Sexuality broadly defined is the capacity for relationship, for ecstasis, for self-transcendence.... Sexual desire and sexual need are a continual contradiction to the illusion that we can exist by ourselves, entirely for ourselves.... At the same time, sexuality is a vital path to holiness, creativity, fecundity, friendship, inclusiveness, delight and pleasure.[3]

Incarnational thinking takes seriously our belief that one of us is God, that human flesh clothed divinity; human feelings and emotions filled his heart, human relationships helped form and transform him. It also places new emphasis on the immanence of God. God is with us, within us. God is not a God who is beyond, transcendent, unreachable. God pitched a tent and lived among us.

The impact of a belief that God incarnated in Jesus is captured by a medieval tale of an abbot who, in frustration over the rankling and bitterness that destroyed life in the community, went to a holy rabbi for advice. The rabbi listened and then told the abbot to gather the monks and tell them that God lived among them. Peace returned when the abbot did as he was told. Monks started treating one another with respect and love. Later, the abbot heard one of the monks telling a visitor, "One of us is God." That belief transformed the life of the community. Because of the incarnation, we can truly sing, "One of us is God."

Prophetic

Jesus was not crucified for healing and consoling people. He was crucified because his teachings were a challenge to oppressive elements in society, especially oppressive elements in the teachings of some Pharisees and other religious leaders. He spoke against laws, customs, and rulers who oppressed people. He welcomed marginalized persons to eat with him and share his company.

Prophets are usually marginal people who see evil and sin in society and speak out against them. They are people who see what others do not see. They live at the cutting edge of society. They are the Isaiahs, Jeremiahs, Pauls, Dorothy Days, and Martin Luther Kings. They are also the women and men in our parishes and neighborhoods who enable us to see the local injustices and oppressions that color everyday existence. They know, as Dorothy Day once said, that "our trouble stems from our acceptance of this filthy rotten system."[4] Prophets awaken the dangerous memory of the challenge of the gospels.

Empowering

Jesus was not about the business of making people dependent upon him. His healing of the blind and the lame enabled them to assume responsibility for their lives and the lives of others. His controversial Sabbath day healing of the woman bent over by disease enabled her to more fully enter into and celebrate Sabbath. Often, after a healing, Jesus issued a challenge: "Sin no more"; "Go show yourself to the priest"; "Take up your bed and walk." The message seems to be, "I have done something great for you. Now it's up to you."

Jean Baker Miller[5] offers some fine insight into the issue of empowerment. She speaks of two kinds of dependence: permanent and temporary. Permanent dependence is for the benefit of the dominant person. Slavery is perhaps the best example of permanent dependence. The relationship exists for the good of the master; the needs of the slave are not considered. It is obvious that this is not a good model for ministry. Temporary dependence, on the other hand, is for the benefit of the person in need. Miller gives as examples the relationships between parents and children, teachers and students. I would suggest ministers and the persons to whom we minister also relate best when the dependence is temporary.

People come to the church in their need. As church, our responsibility is to help them through their problems and enable them to better live a Christian life. On the level of systemic oppression, the church ministers to eliminate hunger, homelessness, and poverty so that the whole society may more easily embrace the fullness of life in God.

Focusing attention on the needs of the persons we serve is not to deny that ministers also benefit from the ministerial relationship. I have sometimes heard ministers talk about feeling good about being able to minister with poor people. And that is a good thing. Ministry is meant to gladden the hearts of all concerned. A problem arises, however, when that good feeling becomes the primary motivation for ministry. Then we lose sight of the responsibility to heal, redeem, and liberate the least of our sisters and brothers.

We do not minister to feel good about ourselves but to do good for others. Experiencing delight in what we do might be an unexpected gift, something extra, but it is not the heart of the matter.

It is important to realize that ministry does not always leave us feeling good. Sometimes, it is hard for people to accept our ministry. Our efforts may make them feel uncomfortable or embarrassed, especially if they are not able to recognize love in what we do. St. Vincent de Paul put it well: "It is only by feeling your love that the poor will be able to forgive you the gift of bread."

Seeing Christ in his Followers

Sacred Scripture is, of course, the sine-qua-non for those who wish to know Jesus, but we can also discover Jesus in the lives of persons faithful to him and his teaching. In the years following the death of St. Francis of Assisi, for example, some of his followers wrote parallel lives of Jesus and Francis. It was a practice they learned from the ancients who used to parallel the lives of great men and Greek gods. It was easy to learn something about Francis in the light of Jesus' life, but it was also easy to learn something about Jesus in the light of Francis' life. Studying Francis meant coming to know Jesus.

That pattern continues today. Robert Krieg, motivated "by the conviction that some types of narratives allow us to know dimensions of personal existence which would elude us if we excluded narratives from our discourse,"[6] presents the life of Dorothy Day as a way of understanding who Jesus is. Her life and work were grounded in faith in Jesus and give us insight into who Jesus is and what he means to faithful disciples. We come to understand the teaching of Jesus by studying her life. We come to know Jesus through her life.

Almost every reference to Mother Teresa, even in the popular media, speaks of her in terms of her fidelity to Jesus. She embodied the "preferential option for the poor" before we had the words to describe it. She, like others less known, gives some insight into Jesus, but of course, no one gives the whole story. We are coming to recognize that, indeed, Christ is risen and lives in all his holy followers.

The Historical Jesus

The search for the historical Jesus of the last two centuries has not produced strong enough evidence for any one particular image. It seems that we have as many different perceptions of Jesus as there are interpreters. Some see him as a zealot, others as the prince of peace. His words have been used to justify war and to demand peace. Not surprisingly, each image of Jesus bears remarkable similarity to the various persons describing him.

As we have already noted, the gospels, the main source of information about the life of Jesus, are not biographies. The evangelists do not provide us with verifiable facts. The gospels are faith statements meant to engender faith in the people for whom they were written. There is enough difference in the reporting of particular scenes to suggest that each evangelist had the needs of the community at heart in the telling of the story of Jesus. The gospels were written, not so that people would know *about* Jesus but that they would come to know *Jesus*. This knowing by faith is what we discussed in chapter one.

Artists Speak of Jesus

There is a statue in the garden of Emmanuel College in Toronto where women meet whenever a woman is abused or murdered in that city. Sculpted by Almuth Lutkenhaus-Lackey, it depicts a broken female body known as the Crucified Woman. The artist enables us to see that the suffering of the crucified Jesus provides insight into the suffering of so many abused women today. The suffering of those women both informs and is informed by the saving cross of Christ. In the same way, Christa, a crucified woman sculpted by Edwina Sandys that hung in New York's Cathedral of St. John the Divine, prompted Dean James Parks Morton to say, in response to criticism of a female Christ, "One is dealing with metaphor, with art. And deep theology, like deep poetry, is not literal stuff."[7]

The Jewish artist Marc Chagall uses the crucifixion to afford new understanding of the Holocaust. A young Jewish man, surrounded by images of Judaism, and of the ghettos to which they were assigned by the Nazis, hangs in anguish. Chagall thus challenges Christians to plumb the depths of the suffering of innocent Jews; he forces Christians to come to grips with the horror of that suffering and of Christian involvement in that suffering. He provides insight into the ongoing crucifixion of Christ in the world in our time.

The brightly colored painting, "Peasants of Solantiname," unites, in Latin style, the suffering of oppressed peasants with that of Jesus. Townspeople are gathered at the foot of the cross upon which hangs a young man. Neither the Crucified Woman nor the Peasants of Solantiname romanticizes suffering; rather they lift up the agony of innocents as it relates to the agony of Jesus. It is not just that a relationship is developed between them: these images speak to Christ suffering today. The abused women, oppressed peasants, and butchered Jews are Christ suffering from the sins of our day. We come to greater sensitivity of the meaning of Christ as each new image provides wisdom into the mystery of Christ. The grace of the artists goes beyond their individual masterpieces. Their images open ways for us to recognize the Crucified One in the terrible sufferings of our day. Many cities and towns have begun to celebrate the stations of the cross on Good Friday by marching through the streets carrying a cross and stopping at appropriate sites for each station. Hospitals, homeless shelters, crack houses, and burned out buildings are thus incorporated into (made one body with) the suffering of Jesus. In such places we may come to discover Christ crucified. As a result, we will probably have a different response to the question, "Were you there when they crucified my Lord?"

Christ in Resurrection

The death of Jesus is not the end of the story. His resurrection is God's "No" to the suffering and death of Jesus. It is the final overcoming of evil by good. The risen Christ reveals God's ultimate inexhaustible love. God raised Jesus to a new and glorious life after the degradation of the cross.

Resurrection is not resuscitation of a corpse, a return to a former life. Resurrection is awakening to new life, to the glorious life of God. The experience of the disciples of the exalted body of Christ, free from the bonds of time and space, vindicated their faith in Jesus, which had been shaken by the horror of his death. It was the lens through which they interpreted the events of his life and understood his teaching. Everything we know of Jesus from the gospels is in the light of the resurrection.

Jesus' resurrection is the promise of our own. When we pray the creed we express our trust that God will be faithful to us even as God was faithful to Jesus. We do not believe that our souls alone will rise but that we will be raised to new life as fully human beings, body and soul. It may be helpful for ministers to emphasize the connection between crucifixion and resurrection in our preaching, teaching, and counseling so that Christians will be able to read the events of their lives in light of resurrection, as they already do with the crucifixion.

Christ in Liturgy

Ask any class of Catholic children preparing for first communion what is meant by the Real Presence and they will tell you that the bread and wine become the Body and Blood of Christ at Mass. They are right, of course, but only partially so. In the Eucharist, Christ is present in the elements of the bread and wine, but also in the presider, in the word proclaimed, and in the gathered assembly. It is Christ himself who celebrates Eucharist. The whole point of the celebration of Eucharist is our incorporation into Christ.

It has been easy for Christians to recognize Christ in the presider, especially because of the solemnity with which the words, "This is my body. . . This is my blood" are surrounded. In the same way, we recognize Christ in the proclamation of the word. But it seems difficult for us to recognize Christ in the assembled community, even though we call ourselves the Mystical Body of Christ.

The church is most church, most Christ at the celebration of Eucharist. At communion, when the minister says, "Body of Christ. . . Blood of Christ," we receive the sacred bread and wine but we also are made aware of the assembled Body of Christ. At Eucharist, the Christian community is incorporated into Christ. We become Christ.

Communion is a vital part of Eucharist, but there is more to Eucharist than that. Eucharist is an action of the community, it is something we do together with the presider. All of the ministers involved in Eucharist, from the welcomers to the choir and lectors, cantors, assistants at table and presider, act for the community. But the rest of the community is not to be passive or silent. We do not "hear Mass," that is, follow what the priest is doing without making any contribution ourselves. The assembled community participates consciously, actively, and fully. Truly, we may say, every Eucharist is concelebrated. Even more than that, because it is an action of Christ the high priest, we may say every Eucharist is celebrated by the Mystical Body of Christ, by the Head and his members together.

SUMMARY

1. Jesus is truly and fully God and truly and fully human. Neither nature is diluted or diminished in the incarnation.

2. The gospels are faith statements about Jesus, written for the benefit of the various communities of followers; they are not history or biography.

3. Jesus, quoting Isaiah, announced his mission to the poor, the blind, the downtrodden; Jesus announced the coming reign of God.

4. The ministry of Jesus might be described as incarnate, prophetic, and empowering. It was always for the good of persons and communities.

5. We can recognize Christ in the lives of those most faithful to his teachings.

6. We recognize the sufferings of Christ in the sufferings of the poor and oppressed today. Artists keep the image vividly before our eyes.

7. The resurrection is God's "no" to the evils imposed on Jesus during his passion. It is a vindication of his life, teachings, and death. The resurrection of Jesus is also a promise of our own resurrection.

8. In the Eucharist, Christ is present in the sacred species, in the presider, in the word, and in the assembly gathered to celebrate.

POINTS FOR REFLECTION

In this chapter we reflected on the ministry of Jesus as incarnate, prophetic, and empowering. What other characteristics would you list?

How can we bring the community to a better understanding that Eucharist is something we do together rather than something we watch the presider do?

What does the artwork on display in your parish (stained glass windows, statues, pictures in the parish office) say about Christ?

How does the parish help people to see Christ in one another, in the community?

What can we learn of Christ from the lives of the people with whom we minister?

CHAPTER FOUR

To Be Human

What we believe about human nature reveals a lot about why we minister. For those who focus on the sinfulness of humanity, ministry is about converting, turning people from sin, perhaps even punishing them for faults and failures. For those who believe in the basic goodness of humanity, however, ministry is about something entirely different. Occasionally, ministers would do well to reflect on their foundational beliefs concerning what it means to be human; that is, on the theological anthropology that undergirds their ministry.

In God's Image

Having already said that God saturates our world and all of creation, I have tipped my hand about what I believe about what it means to be human. Created in God's image, temple of the Holy Spirit, Body of Christ—what more profound metaphors can the church supply for our understanding of who we are? It seems Christians have been so focused on personal sin for such a long time that we have lost sight of the magnificence of the good news of God's love for us. God loves us; therefore we are lovable. If we could only really rely on that truth, how our lives might change. Each of us might sing with the psalmist,

> Truly, you have formed my inmost being;
> you knit me in my mother's womb.
> I give you thanks that I am fearfully, wonderfully made;
> Wonderful are your works. (Psalm 139)

Our Capacity for God

Human beings are not the opposite of God, being all that God is not. Human beings are oriented toward God by their very nature. To be human is to have a longing for God, a capacity for God, an orientation toward God. The essence of what it means to be human is determined by that orientation. Elizabeth Johnson beautifully describes that orientation as having an infinite capacity for truth, for love, and for life.[1]

The capacity for truth is evident in the toddler's "why...why...why?" and in the scholar's arduous pursuit of deeper and more profound truth. Newspapers, magazines, radio, and television, to say nothing of the internet, stand in stark witness to the human urge toward truth. The more we know, the more there is to know. Each answer leads to deeper and more profound questions. This is as evident in the field of theology as it is in the field of science. The capacity for truth appears infinite.

Only God can fill that capacity for truth.

No one says, "I have used up all my ability to love. I cannot love any more persons than I already do," or "I love you so much that I could never grow in love, never love you more." The love of spouses is not threatened by the love they have for their children. Loving persons constantly reach out to others, love urging them on to greater and greater love. Communities of love constantly reach out to include more and more persons. For many, the experience of being loved awakens in them the ability to love. The capacity for love appears infinite.

Only God can fill that capacity for love.

The ability to imagine and hope in the midst of the most terrible situations has been witnessed to by survivors of the Holocaust and by victims of violence, oppression, and war around the globe. Tales of systemic abuse and of excruciating pain are often simply background for the notes of hope that sustain victims. Anne Frank, keeping the flame of hope alive in her crowded attic hiding place, wrote, "And in the evening, when I lie in bed and end my prayers with the words, 'I thank you God, for all that is good and dear and beautiful.' ...I don't think then of all the misery, but of the beauty that still remains."[2] Hope against hope enables people to trust that life can and will be better. Christians speak of this trust as reliance on God, knowing that God will not abandon us, no matter how desperate the situation. The capacity for hope and for life appears infinite. Hope, as the poet says, is eternal.

Hope, as we are discussing it here, is a theological virtue. It is not to be confused with optimism or with a cheerful personality. Hope is a deep conviction that God can be trusted, that God will be faithful to promises, and that God wills only what is good for us. According to Richard McBrien, "Hope is grounded in faith—in a faith that sees creation and history as guided and protected always by the healing hand of God, and in a faith in the promises of God that in the end the Kingdom will be given in all its fullness."[3]

Only God can fill that capacity for hope.

We might add the compelling magnetism of beauty as a capacity for the infinite.

We can repeat, with Augustine, "Too late have I loved you, O Beauty so ancient yet ever new! Too late have I loved you! And, behold, you were within me and I out of myself, and there I searched for You."[4] So often we miss that ancient beauty incarnate in our world because we searched for beauty in ways and places that hardly leave room for true beauty, so full of narcissism and selfishness are some standards of beauty today. The standard of beauty set by systems intent on making money or attaining power over others is not what is meant by beauty here.

Beauty is not about appearances but rather about the ability of creation and of human creations in their myriad manifestations, to warm the heart, excite passions, impel toward goodness and truth. Beauty is goodness so deep and profound as to move the human heart toward God. Andrew Greeley mourns that because we do not attend enough to the beautiful, the dominant style of ministry is still authoritarian pragmatism. "We constrain people to be virtuous," he says. "While the enforcers are different from the monsignori and mothers superior of an earlier age, the method used today by lay and ordained ministers has not changed."[5]

To be human is to be mystery searching for truth, for love, for life, and for beauty. The mystery of finite humanity is, in Johnson's words, "[that] we are dynamically structured toward God and will only be satisfied by the infinite God."[6] Augustine's poetic, "You have made us for yourself, O God, and our hearts are restless until they rest in

You," has withstood the amnesia of the ages to remind us of this truth.

The ache of the human spirit is for the divine mystery that is Truth, Love, Life, and Beauty. Ministry is one of the ways Christians have devised to help ease that ache. Various education programs for children and adults, retreats, parish food pantries, and well-prepared liturgies— these all have their beginning and end in the mystery of God. Offering the community the opportunity to approach truth, embrace love, rejoice in hope, and experience beauty is to touch the divine mystery.

Grace

Sometimes we speak of grace and nature as if they are separate entities. The old adage "Grace builds on nature" leaves some of us thinking that nature is somehow apart from grace. There is no such thing as ungraced nature. From the first moment of our existence, we are graced, in relationship with God. Hildegarde of Bingen has a beautiful painting that clearly illustrates her conviction of this. At the bottom of a long panel is a pregnant woman. The umbilical cord twines through a lattice filled with flowers and butterflies and birds as it winds its way up to the Trinity. The life of God flows to the baby in the mother's womb through the umbilical cord. The life of God flowed to us in our mother's womb. Our conception in our parents' act of love is the sign and sacrament of the passionate love of God, and so is graced.

Grace, God's life, is not apart from nature. Genesis records that, at creation, God took stuff of the earth and breathed on it. Only then did human life come to be. That creation myth is not about some ancient event; it is a way of describing God's ongoing activity in human creation. God takes stuff of the earth (our parents' love and bodies) and breathes divine life into that stuff to create new life.

To be human, then, is to be in relationship with God. Every human being is sustained by the breath of God. Every human being is image and likeness of God. Every human being is fundamentally oriented toward God. There is no such thing as ungraced nature. Grace presupposes the nature of human person; human nature includes the capacity for grace.

This does not mean that we always recognize grace. In fact, says Karl Rahner, "...the possibility of experiencing grace and the possibility of experiencing grace as grace are not the same thing."[7] There is no dualism involved here; nature supposes grace. Grace is not something extra bestowed on a chosen few or earned by prayer and sacrifice. As Leonardo Boff has put it so beautifully, "Nothing in human beings fails to be loved and permeated by God."[8]

Human Response to the Holy

Important as it is to emphasize God's self-communication, we need also to turn our attention to the human response to that communication. There are moments in life that may be defined as depth experiences, experiences that put us in touch with God. These experiences of ordinary life can touch the soul so deeply that we are able to recognize divinity in the moment. It may be a beautiful symphony, a deep sharing of friendship, awesome natural beauty—all considered "secular" experiences. But any experience that awakens the soul to truth, love, life, and beauty is truly religious. The church's involvement in justice and peace endeavors is religious. Promotion of the arts is religious. Healing broken bodies is religious.

Of course, experiences of the holy in prayer, reflection, the sacraments, and the like are depth experiences that, as ministers, we may help provide for the people of God. The hunger and thirst for God that are so evident in our society demand that liturgies be graceful and grace-filled events and that homilies be well prepared and delivered. This hunger and thirst demands that the community we foster and support be founded in justice and compassion. It demands that love be the bedrock of all ministries. But, as Dorothy Day contends, love is not enough. In her autobiography, she describes a year that she spent at Kings County Hospital as a student nurse. One of the patients, a 94-year-old woman, fought with the nurses and would not accept their ministrations. One of the nurses said, "Can't you see we want to take care of you because we love you?" The response was "Love be damned, I want my wig." Fortunately, a nurse who "had sympathy and understanding realized that the little old lady needed more than soap and water and clean bed linens. She needed more than to be loved. She needed to be respected as a person, and for that, she needed to have her wishes respected. She needed such appurtenances as her wig. I remember we compromised with a cap and so pleased her."[9]

Failures in Love

As I suggested earlier, because of an over-emphasis on sin in the recent past, I believe it is necessary to focus attention on such positive understandings of human nature as we have just discussed. It would be a serious mistake, however, to ignore the myriad manifestations of sin that we encounter every day. We are the image of God; we are graced from the first moment of conception; we are God's beloved. But we are also sinners who forget all that. Because we forget, we lie, cheat, exploit, distort, and violate; we are unfaithful; we are selfish.

Sin, then, is the rupture of a relationship with God. At its core, sin defiles that relationship and relationships with other persons and with all of creation, as we learn from the Genesis story. The myth known as "The Fall" is not a historical account of what happened to two persons at the dawn of creation. It is a vision of the effects of our sin in the here and now. The import of the creation myth is that sin affected the relationship between the man and woman, and between them and God, and left destructive marks on all of creation. Sin is never merely private and personal. The effects of sin may be likened to the proverbial and mythic butterfly that flaps its wings in Tokyo and causes a thunderstorm in New York.

Making the Abstract Real

Thus far, we have been discussing humanity in the abstract. It is easy to love humanity in the abstract. But in our parishes, we find human beings, women and men, in the flesh. Then our love is put to the test. In order to truly love and serve the people of God, we must first know the community, its needs, its hopes, and its fears. Serving the community means putting its needs, hopes, and fears first, rather than coming with the answer to problems that we may think are the most important.

This came home to me in a dramatic way when I spent some time in India. The Indian government, in an effort to improve the life in the poorest villages, set aside money to build a well in each village. Such wells, it was thought, would make life easier for the village women–the traditional bearers of well water; the wells would provide clean water for all and improve both the health and economic conditions of the village. A problem arose when one village, which already had a fine working well, appealed instead for the money to provide soap and shoes for the children. The people of the village argued that soap and shoes would reduce infections and illnesses among the children and avoid unnecessary duplication. The government, however, proved adamant. Wells it would be, or nothing.

Not all needs are material. One of my students shared an experience he had in Chile when a new sister came to his mission. She brought funds from generous supporters and, seeing the long walk the women had to make each morning to the well–and the even harder walk back home balancing heavy jugs of water on their heads–suggested that a well be dug in the middle of the village. The women of the town objected and called for building a school for their children. After the new school opened, the sister, thinking that the women had sacrificed their own comfort for their children, again suggested digging a well.

One afternoon over coffee, the women finally felt free to speak their concerns. "Going to and from the well is the only time we have with one another, the only time husbands and children are not calling on us," they told her. "This is precious time we have with one another."

When Mahatma Gandhi was asked what definite work missionaries should do among the people, he replied,

"The spinning wheel."[10] Gandhi understood that the production of homespun "khadi" affirmed the dignity of labor by providing jobs and offering some economic resistance to colonialism, which required India to provide cotton for British fabric mills. It also reaffirmed Indian culture and tradition. The seeds of a solution lay within the people themselves.

Whether or not Gandhi meant that literally (and he may have), I believe that he was saying that we must know the struggles of the people and join them in their solutions, rather than impose ideas from outside the community. Whatever the problem of a community, the solution is already hidden deep within that community.

Scripture provides us with many models for leaders of communities who spoke and ministered from deep within the community. Not the least of these is Martha, beloved of Jesus,[11] who led the Johannine community through a crisis of faith concerning Jesus' promise that anyone who followed him would never die. Martha expresses the faith of the community in Jesus, even as Peter does in the synoptic gospels. She knows the people well enough to express that faith in various ways so that all would understand. She calls Jesus the Messiah (recognized by the Jews), the Son of God (understood by the Gentiles), and the One Who is to come (a phrase used by the Samaritans).

Knowing Your People

Leaders of all stripes, but especially Christian leaders, need to be well rooted in the community. For Christian leaders, this is a sure sign that they have faith in the Spirit alive and dynamic in the people. Trusting the work of the

Spirit in the community means being able to recognize the gifts and talent that are available there. It means being able to spark those gifts so that they may grow and set the fire of the gospel aglow among the community.

Paul Mundey[12] suggests that not knowing a congregation's culture may lead to acts of violence against that culture. To avoid that violence, he suggests getting to know the community's symbols, language, values, narrative, and history—in other words, to be deeply involved in the life of the community. In addition, Mundey cautions ministers to be aware of the forces of the greater culture and the influence of the particular denomination on the life of the parish.

Trust, Translate, Turbo-charge

A three-pronged formula for affirming and reapplying that religious heritage is offered by Leonard Sweet: trust your tradition, translate your tradition, and turbo-charge your tradition.[13] This may be another way of saying that people need both roots and wings. The deep roots of our tradition are meant to enrich the faith of the community. Our rich heritage calls us to fidelity to the teachings of Jesus. It also calls us to live the gospel in our day even as our ancestors in the faith found ways to live the gospel in theirs.

But we are not called to mere imitation of Christians of another age. We are called to translate the tradition faithfully so it may be understood and embraced by the people of our time. In this way, tradition is kept alive and does not become a fossil from the past to be inspected and reverenced but not lived. Understood in this way, tradition, like faith, is a verb, not a noun.

As we saw back in chapter one, the theologians of Vatican II expressed the connection between trusting and translating tradition thus:

> This tradition that comes from apostles develops in the church with the help of the Holy Spirit. For there is a growth in the understanding of the realities and the words which have been handed down.... For as the centuries succeed one another, the church constantly moves forward toward fullness of divine truth until the words of God reach their complete fulfillment in her. (*Dei Verbum*, 8)

As I understand it, turbo-charging tradition involves communicating the message vitally, moving it in the direction of relevancy. It is a challenge to keep alive the fire, the passion of the gospels. We shortchange the gospel and the Christian community when sentimental versions of the Good News are all that is available. Jesus was not crucified for telling people to be kind and gentle with one another. He was crucified because of the fire and passion of his teaching.

Every Christian a Minister

The pastoral staff does not have to personally respond to every need they encounter. They need, rather, to engage enough parishioners to minister to the needs of all. Of course, that means knowing the community, knowing who has a healing touch and may serve the sick and dying, knowing who is able to preach the word, knowing who understands the language of the young, knowing whose life experience enables them to counsel and console. The whole community is in need of ministry; the whole community ministers.

The book of Exodus records an event in the life of Moses that gets lost among the stories of the wonders that accompanied the Hebrews across the desert. It seems that Moses had set up a system whereby the people could have their disagreements settled and receive his advice, which they took as coming from God. When Jethro, his father-in-law, visited, he noticed some problems that had escaped the attention of Moses. The people had to wait in line "from morning to night" to get their hearing, and Moses was unnecessarily wearing himself out. "You are not acting wisely," Jethro said to Moses. "You will surely wear yourself out, and not only yourself but also these people with you. The task is too heavy for you alone; you cannot do it alone" (Ex 18:14–18). Jethro advised Moses to choose trustworthy, God-fearing leaders to assist in the task. "Thus your burden will be lightened, since they will bear it with you. If you do this, when God gives you orders, you will be able to stand the strain and all these people will go home satisfied" (Ex 18:22–23).

This is a message for today. None of us has to do it alone. None of us has to carry the burden by ourselves. None of us has a monopoly on talent and ability.

There is no reason for parish ministers to try to do it alone. The parish is full of baptized women and men who, by virtue of that baptism, have received sacramental grace for ministry. Parishes that have expanded ministries to include these parishioners find themselves more vibrant and responsive to the needs of the church and the world.

SUMMARY

1. Human beings are created in the very image of God, having an infinite capacity for Truth, Love, Life, and Beauty.

2. Human beings are graced from the first moment of their existence. There is no such thing as ungraced nature.

3. Sin is a rupture in our relationship with God. It is both personal and systemic.

4. Ministers need to be deeply involved in the life of the community, knowing its symbols, values, narrative, and history.

5. Baptism calls every Christian to ministry. Parish ministers may foster and support these ministries, thereby enabling greater response to the needs of the church and the world and helping to bring about the reign of God.

POINTS FOR REFLECTION

How does the teaching that all human beings are graced from the first moment of existence affect what we teach about baptism?

What effort does the parish make to help fill the human capacity for Truth, Love, Hope, and Beauty?

Andrew Greeley maintains that we constrain people to be virtuous rather than appeal to the human longing for beauty. In what ways might the parish draw people to God through beauty?

How would you describe to a youth group the concept of sin as fracturing a relationship with God?

Think of one problem that exists in your community. What solutions to that problem might already exist within the parish?

CHAPTER FIVE

Church

It is difficult to get people to agree on what they mean by the word "church." But there does seem to be agreement on two points: the church must be rooted in tradition and, at the same time, responsive to the needs of each age. To understand church today, then, it may be well to look at what we know of the early church and the church through the ages. The needs of our own time are only too obvious for all but the most unseeing.

New Testament

Jesus left no blueprint for all times. What we find in the gospels are not rules and regulations or particular structures. We look to Jesus and the early church for inspiration, for values. There is no indication that Jesus thought he was establishing an institution that would last until the twenty-first century and beyond. He focused his attention on the daily pain and suffering of the people he met. He condemned powerful persons and institutions that exploited the poor. He sent his disciples throughout the countryside to heal and liberate in his name.

It may seem ironic that the only structure Jesus established, the Twelve, disappeared a few years after his death. There was only one attempt to maintain a body of twelve as the recognized leaders–when Matthias was chosen to replace Judas. The number twelve, of course, held great meaning for the Jews. Choosing twelve leaders, Jesus set his community in the context of the twelve tribes of Israel. Perhaps the number twelve, so significant in the history of the Jews, was not so mystical for the many Gentile converts and so fell into disuse.

In her classic work, *In Memory of Her,* Elisabeth Schüsssler Fiorenza describes the community around Jesus as "the discipleship of equals." Many familiar sayings of Jesus, including "The first shall be last" and "I do not call you servants but friends," as well as the meals shared with sinners, outcasts, and poor persons, highlight the expectations Jesus had for those who followed him.

Each of the gospels and the Acts of the Apostles, along with other manuscripts available from those times, witness to a particular way of being a disciple. In Jerusalem, James, along with elders, led the community. John's community appears to have operated in a less structured way.

Matthew is thought to have been written for a predominantly Jewish community, while Luke addresses a mostly Gentile group of converts. The needs of each community determined the way stories about Jesus were recounted and what lessons were drawn from them.

Because the needs of each community shaped the way we see Christ, we need to take seriously a warning Eugene Maly gave in a report to the American bishops. "From what has been said," he noted, it should be evident that we can expect to find in the scriptures an evolution in the concept of ministry that is eminently in keeping with the nature of a pilgrim people of God. . . It will mean, first of all, that we cannot use the old testament as a primary referent for our conception of Christian ministry. . .

Acceptance of the concept of evolution will mean, secondly, that even in the new testament we should not expect to find a clearly formulated definition of Christian ministry from the beginning, or at any simple single point in the development of new testament revelation. Christian ministry was never frozen in any one mold but continued to develop and be adapted in succeeding moments in history. This does not mean that there is no normative character to the new testament canon. But the normative character will not be seen in definitive "canonizing" of one exercise of ministry without regard for another, or of one historical manifestation at one time or place in isolation from other such manifestations. Development itself is canonical and therefore normative.[1]

A Changing Church

Karl Rahner argued that the church has had only three distinct periods of history, three epochs that are so different and distinct from one another that the Christians of an earlier era cannot recognize the church of the later one.[2] The first era, that of Jewish Christianity, lasted only a short time—from Pentecost to the great influx of Gentile converts. Pity the poor Jewish followers who followed the Way of Christ but still went to the Temple and kept the dietary laws. The face of the church they knew changed so radically that they could not recognize it. What could they make of all the innovations that came about as Gentiles came to hear about the teachings and life of Jesus and to respond to that teaching and life from their own culture? It took a Greek imagination to develop the dogmas of the Trinity and the divinity of Christ. Early Jewish Christians, radically monotheistic, would have had to struggle with these strange concepts. The contributions of the Greeks could only have astounded them.

The second epoch lasted into the twentieth century. No matter the problems and fractures encountered throughout history, the church could still be recognized by old-timers. The East-West schism and the Reformation notwithstanding, the rites, creeds, and mores could be relied on. The church had taken on a Hellenistic/European flavor, and its changes mirrored the culture in which it existed. Developments in the church paralleled developments in the greater society and so were not terribly disconcerting to most Christians. One generation was not very different from another. Cultures were more fixed over time; customs lasted more than a few years. The church of children and grandchildren was still the church their grandparents knew.

Vatican II marks the ecclesial boundary for the third age. Opening the windows of the church, Pope John XXIII inaugurated a time for the church to redefine itself in the light of new knowledge, both secular and religious. He saw the church as a catalyst for such knowledge, and sent a message for the bishops of the council to approve and sign saying, "we look forward to a spiritual renewal from which also will flow a happy impulse on behalf of human values such as scientific discoveries, technological advances, and a wider diffusion of knowledge."[3] His was to be a positive council, not declaring condemnations—as many past councils had done—but celebrating what was grace in society and in the church. The tone was set. That positive tone emerged from a sacramental sense. If the church is to be easily recognized as sacrament of God, it must be as God is—merciful.

Living at the beginning of the third age and taking seriously the metaphor "people of God," we are all challenged to find remarkably innovative ways to be church. Advances in communication and transportation contribute to new (and for some, frightening) changes in the church. News flashes around the world as it is happening. The trials and joys of all have become our trials and joys. "Neighbor" has been stretched to include persons dispossessed by natural disasters in far flung locales as well as those who live among us.

Church in the Third World

In 1978 Walbert Buhlmann[4] accurately forecast what we are now observing. The center of gravity of the church is moving to the continents of Asia, Africa, and South America.

Asian, African, and Latin American theologies, liturgies, and practices are defining the church anew. Following the insights available to them, missionaries in the past transplanted Eurocentric versions of Christianity on other continents. But that no longer suffices. Missionaries today are involved in inculturation, a process that respects the religious traditions of a people by transforming the culture from within rather than imposing practices and beliefs from without. In the sixteenth century Matteo Ricci, S.J., learned to live and think like the Chinese in order to introduce Christianity from within that culture. In India,

Roberto de Nobili learned to live and think like a Hindu, and from that perspective was able to root the church in the culture of the people. Both men were vilified in their day but are taken as models for missionary activity today.

The music and art of these cultures enrich and enliven their liturgies. But these may be only cosmetic changes. The religious traditions of non-European cultures are bringing new insights to the gospel message. Some of the most exciting and challenging theology is being developed by theologians from developing countries.

This coming of the third church is marked by populations that are younger and poorer than in the so-called developed world. For better or for worse, the church looks and will continue to look different on different continents and even among the various peoples on each continent. Diversity in unity marks the third worldwide church.

Major cities around the world have become microcosms of our planet. People from every continent rub elbows at school and at work. In church, we rub elbows and minds and hearts. God has found another way to reveal divinity to us. God is present in the women and men, black and white, red and yellow, gay and straight, rich and poor who fill our pews. Truly, we can echo James Joyce, who, when asked what "Catholic" meant, replied, "Here comes everybody."

Church as Sacrament

Of all the ways Vatican II described the church, the primary understanding presented was the church as sacrament or mystery or, as Pope Paul VI put it, "a reality imbued with the hidden presence of God." While the church in a unique and radical way is imbued with the hidden presence of God, our reflection in chapter two suggested that all of creation is saturated with that holy presence. The pope's careful use of the article "a" rather than the more particular "the" suggests that the church is not the only reality that is sacramental or revelatory of God.

Ocean waves and mountain peaks, squirrels and daisies, all the wonders of nature speak of God. The birth of a baby and the death of a loved one also speak of God. Loving friends and kind neighbors tell of God. When the church speaks out against injustice, we may more easily recognize God. When the church acts against systems that oppress, we may more easily recognize God. Of course, when the church comes together to pray, especially when we come together to celebrate Eucharist, God is in our midst and made more easily recognizable. Here, as in the rest of the discussion about church, I am not merely speaking of the institutional structure of the church, such as the bishops and pope. I am not excluding them, either. The church is responsible for being sacrament of God—and that means all of us.

Tragic Sacraments of God

It is not only in the glorious moments of life that God is present. I am reminded of Nobel Prize winner Elie Wiesel's story of a hanging that all the prisoners in a concentration camp were forced to watch. One of the persons being executed was a young boy who did not weigh enough to pull on the noose. He hung alive long after the two men hanged with him had died. One of the prisoners screamed, "Where is God?" only to be answered with, "Here He is—He is hanging here on this gallows."[5] God is present even in tragedy, illness, and sorrow. It may be more difficult to recognize the divine presence there but our blindness does not exile God from these human events.

The splendor of God is so breathtaking we are not able to live through that direct experience of God. We do not experience God immediately; rather, as we have seen, God's self-revelation is mediated by all of creation. But that revelation occurs in a special and profound way in the church. We might think of the church as that part of creation established, consecrated, and committed to reveal God to the world but also to truly make God present in the world.

Although the church, like the rest of creation, makes God present in a somewhat veiled way, it is a way that makes God more easily perceived. At the same time, the church, composed as it is of human beings who sin, is itself involved in sin and may distort God's presence. Sacrament that it is, the church is nevertheless always in need of reformation.

The church's nature as sacramental is evident in myriad ways. We will discuss only three of those ways here. They are: our penchant for celebration, our devotion to the saints, and our commitment to social justice.

Penchant for Celebrating

Sacramentality marks Catholics, both as individuals and communities. We use the stuff of the earth in our liturgies, rituals, and celebrations of everyday life. We wave palms, mark with ashes, dunk in water, anoint with oil, and lift up bread and wine to be changed into the Body and Blood of Christ. The stuff of the earth does not get in the way but rather opens us to God in our midst. The psalmist sings the glory of creation:

The heavens tell of your glory, O God,
And the skies proclaim your handiwork;
one day tells the next day,
night passes on the knowledge to night. (Psalm 19)

We are a people who know how to celebrate. Protestant church historian Martin Marty claims that Catholics have never feared the ecstacy of the dance. Think of the art and music that have been created through the ages. Think of the majesty of the Easter liturgy or of Midnight Mass at Christmas. Recall the pageantry of papal celebrations broadcast around the world. We appeal to every sense in our liturgies. The flickering light of candles, the smell of incense, the sound of music, the touch of a neighbor's hand, and the taste of communion all speak of God.

So sacramental are we that we are sometimes criticized for being too earthy, carnal, sensual, even bawdy. In our celebration of the gifts of creation, we do sometimes get lost in our own exuberance. The celebration of Mardi Gras, St. Patrick's Day parades, ethnic street festivals, and fiestas took a Catholic imagination and culture to develop. At their best, they shout, as God did upon beholding creation, "It is good."

Poet Hilaire Belloc captures what I have been trying to say here:

Where e'er the Catholic sun doth shine
There's music and laughter and good red wine.
At least I've always found it so,
Benedicamus Domino![6]

Communion of Saints

Our catalogue of saints, whether canonized and not, is another tribute to the church's sacramental nature. We can detect God's presence in one another. So enamored are we of the idea of relating with these holy souls that we celebrate the "feast of splendid nobodies."[7] All Saints Day gives us the opportunity to honor and celebrate our own personal saints—Grandma and Uncle Joe, the martyrs of El Salvador, housewives and truck drivers, athletes and everyday heroes. The communion of saints, so dear to the Catholic heart, is rooted in sacramentality, finding God sometimes in surprising places and shocking persons. Saints include gentle humble persons, courageous prophets, and whimsical eccentrics. Among them are Christians, Jews, Moslems, and all sorts of other believers and non-believers. "The friends of God and prophets," writes Elizabeth Johnson, "are found in every nation and tongue, culture and religion, and even among religion's cultured despisers."[8] Catholics do not have a monopoly on sainthood. We do, however, seem to have a unique appreciation for the relationship that exists between all the living and those who have already passed into eternal life.

When we are in need, we pray to saints to ask them to pray for us. St. Anthony will find lost articles, St. Joseph a new home, and St. Jude will take care of the most impossible cases. These devotions are not part of some patronage system, suggesting that God is unapproachable, even indifferent to our prayers and only responsive to a few special friends. They are rather, an indication of the deeply held belief that we and the saints in heaven are part of the community we reverently call the communion of saints.

Just as we ask friends and family to pray for us and we promise to pray for them, we ask the saints in heaven to join those prayers. We are related to one another. The saints care for us because of that relationship.

Some of our saints may be an embarrassment in today's sophisticated and technological era. Taking the folklore surrounding the life of a saint in another era too literally may lead to misunderstanding her or his life. What is needed is a sense of the poetic, a creative imagination that appreciates that there is more to reality than can be expressed in mere words. Seeing what is behind some of the hagiography allows a view of a person living in relationship with God. That relationship is the essence of sanctity.

Commitment to Social Justice

The church's social justice teachings grow out of its nature as sacrament. It is a response to those situations where the presence of God is blurred or distorted. Poverty, prejudice, and oppression are antithetical to the Kingdom of God of which Jesus spoke. The Kingdom of God is not some utopian land of political or social perfection. That Kingdom is none other than Godself. Feeding the hungry, clothing the naked, providing housing for people without shelter are among the ways the church makes God more recognizable and helps bring about that blessed kingdom. By serving the poor and striving to eliminate systems that oppress, we bring God's life among us.

In our day, the bishops of the United States challenge us to make a preferential option for the poor. This does not only mean that we should contribute to the needs of poor persons. It means that we count the effect of our actions, personal and political, on the poor. Even more than that, it means that we become aware of God's preferential option for the poor. God is revealed in potent, if somewhat perplexing ways, in poor people. Homeless families, abused children, exploited workers, all reveal something of God if we only attune ourselves to hearing and seeing that revelation.

Ministry to people who are suffering has a long history in our church, but in recent years we have become aware of the systemic aspect of evil and have committed ourselves as church to eradicate structural sin. We are like the folks in a small village who day after day pulled drowning people from the river and who finally realized that maybe they should go upstream to find out who or what was *throwing them in* the river. Ministry in the cause of justice, then, has two facets: *caring* for persons who suffer and *transforming* systems that oppress; pulling people from the waters of poverty and going upstream to discover the causes of that poverty. Throughout its history, the church responded to the needs of the times as it recognized them with the wisdom of each time. What we are doing in our day is not, therefore, as new and innovative as we might think. Following the wisdom of our age, we as church become more profound sacraments of God as we serve those whom Jesus identified as serving him.

The political and scientific wisdom of our age also impels us to struggle against the devastation of the earth— whether that devastation comes slowly by pernicious pollution or rapidly by destructive nuclear arms. But political or scientific problems are also religious problems. The Christian respect for life in all its forms challenges us to preserve creation not only for ourselves but for the non-human population and for yet unborn generations. As we lead communities in the singing of lyrics like "Let us build the City of God," we are enabling those communities to realize our responsibility as Christians to bring about the reign of God that Jesus preached.

SUMMARY

1. The church is not restricted to the hierarchy. They, with all of us believers, constitute the church.

2. Karl Rahner suggests that there are three distinct epochs in the history of the church: The short period of Jewish Christianity, the almost two-thousand-year period of Hellenistic/European Christianity, and the period upon which we are now embarking, the world church.

3. The church in Africa, the church in Asia, and the church in Latin America are contributing to the life of the entire church. Theologies developed on these continents are presenting challenges to theologies developed in more developed countries.

4. The church is a sacrament of God. Our penchant for celebration, our devotion to the communion of saints, and our commitment to social justice all grow out of the sacramentality of the church.

POINTS FOR REFLECTION

How would you describe your parish to a visitor?

How are we preparing people for the challenges of the "Third Church"? For diversity in unity?

Review how symbols are used in parish celebrations. Are symbols used generously and lavishly? What efforts are used to help people understand the symbols?

Create your own litany of saints. Include family, friends, parishioners, church and civic leaders, and heroes.

How does the parish make the church's "preferential option for the poor" alive for parishioners? What more might be done?

CHAPTER SIX

Who Are Called to Minister?

Lots of people spend their lives doing good for others. Politicians, doctors, police officers, teachers, artists, poets, farmers—the list goes on and on. Not many of these people call what they do "ministry." We might know keenly effective counselors, extraordinary teachers, or altruistic servants of the poor who do not refer to their work as ministry. Yet, the church teaches that all baptized Christians are called to ministry and that the sacraments of ministry are baptism and confirmation. Every Christian is called, by virtue of being baptized, to serve the least of Christ's sisters and brothers.

We might ask how our world would be different if Christians understood that their daily work was truly ministry, if their motivation were service to the world rather than making money or getting ahead? What might the world look like if the church emphatically preached that everything a Christian does in and for the name of Christ to bring about God's reign is ministry?

That does not mean all Christians are called to ecclesial ministry, the internal ministries that keep the church afloat. For ecclesial ministers—lay and ordained—ministry takes on an additional patina, another meaning. Catholics hear a great deal about ministry these days, but in previous decades that word belonged to Protestants. Catholics had priests and sisters and brothers who did what had to be done in the church. While they did not call priests "ministers," they did speak of priests doing ministry; and of sisters and brothers having an apostolate. Of course, the Altar Society and the St. Vincent de Paul Society made wonderful contributions to the parish and beyond, but we did not think of them as ministries. Even the original *Documents of Vatican II* edited by Walter Abbott, S.J.,[1] lists "see clergy, priests" under "minister" in the index.

While I believe we have not yet fully realized the impact of this understanding of baptism proposed by Vatican II, we have begun to experience a significant shift in the life of the church. The bishops and theologians of the Council could not have imagined the impact their words would have on the Catholic community. In presenting baptism as the sacrament of ministry, they set the stage for a radical transformation of the church.

> Incorporated into Christ's Mystical Body through baptism and strengthened by the power of the Holy Spirit through confirmation, they [the laity] are assigned to the apostolate by the Lord himself.

In an earlier age, the ecclesial work of the laity was referred to as "Catholic Action," a title given it by Pope Pius XII. Catholic Action was defined as "participation of laity in the apostolate of the hierarchy." The distinction is significant: the laity helped the hierarchy with their work. Ministry belonged to the ordained.

A few years later, the Second Vatican Council's Decree on the Laity taught that the lay apostolate is a participation in the saving mission of the church itself. "Through their baptism and confirmation, all are commissioned to the apostolate by the Lord himself." Listen to the words, "commissioned by the Lord himself." By the sacraments of baptism and confirmation we are entrusted with the mission of the church, we are called to ministry by the Lord.

Baptism and confirmation commission us to ministry, demand that we minister. Ministry is constitutive of what it means to be Christian.

On the fifteenth anniversary of the Decree on the Laity the U.S. bishops issued a pastoral letter called "The Laity: Called and Gifted," in which they said that one of the chief characteristics of all men and women today is a growing sense of being adult members of the same church. They described laymen and laywomen as feeling themselves called to "exercise the same mature independence and particular self direction which characterize them in other areas of life."[2] While much of the letter is descriptive of the development of lay ministry, the bishops reiterate:

> The adult character of the people of God flows from Baptism and Confirmation which are the foundations of the Christian life and ministry. . . Baptism and Confirmation empower all believers to share in some form of ministry.[3]

These words are not a description of what is happening; they are prescriptive, corrective. They call for what ought to be. <u>Ministers today, like all pioneers, are caught between what was and what will be, in a way unique to our time.</u>

On another anniversary of the Decree on the Laity, this time the thirtieth, the bishops wrote "Called and Gifted for the Third Millennium," reenforcing the message about lay responsibility for the church.

> For our part we bishops cannot imagine ourselves entering a new millennium, embarked on a new evangelization, unless we walk side by side with our lay sisters and brothers. For together we stand at the threshold of a "great venture, both challenging and wonderful. . . reevangelization so much needed by the present world" (*Christifideles Laici,* no. 64).[4]

In the past, change occurred slowly, often over centuries. The pace of transportation and communication slowed the rush of change. Not so today. The internet, satellites, supersonic jets, and the like have transformed us into a global village. "Neighbor" and "community" have been stretched to new meanings, including persons we will never meet face to face. Theologians from developing countries have challenged us to see and respond to poverty and oppression that we might have ignored in the past.

Toward a Definition of Ministry

It is difficult to get much agreement about the meaning of the word "ministry." For some it means almost any good work that any person does. Richard McBrien,[5] following the lead of Yves Congar, presents four categories by which we may speak of ministry. They are general universal, general specific, Christian universal, and Christian specific.

General universal ministry is that service done for others by virtue of our common humanity. In this sense, every human being is called to ministry. *General specific* ministry is that special service performed by virtue of a person's competence. Included are medical professionals, legal aid personnel, social workers, and others whose focus of work is the alleviation of pain and suffering of others.

Christian universal ministry is that ministry to which every baptized person is called. It is service that is carried out in response to the teaching of Jesus and from Christian motivation. *Christian specific* ministry is service rendered *"in the name of the church and for the sake of helping the church fulfill its mission."*[6]

This book is concerned about this last category; ministry that grows out of the competence of the minister and that requires designation by the church. By designation I do not mean only the action of a pastor or bishop, although that is, of course, included. Also included are those acts of ministry that spring from such things as prayer groups and other organizations of Christians whose motivation is to spread the Good News of Jesus Christ. We might think here of such groups as Pax Christi and Call to Action, lay groups committed to the church and to the preaching of the Good News.

Some people count every act of kindness as ministry. They call ministry the generous care and love bestowed by parents on their children, or the neighborly helping hand. For others, ministry refers only to the work done by bishops, pastors, and those commissioned by them.

Thomas O'Meara offers a definition for ministry that

falls somewhere between those two and which may be helpful here. "Christian ministry," he suggests, "is the public activity of a baptized follower of Jesus Christ flowing from the Spirit's charism and an individual personality on behalf of a Christian community to witness to, serve, and realize the kingdom of God."[7]

Each of these criteria needs to be explored. Ministers take seriously the human condition; they serve to answer a need in the community. The public character of ministry suggests that ministers do for persons outside their circle of intimacy what they do for family and friends. The circle of love is expanded. Some may take offense at excluding the loving and generous service to loved ones under the rubric of "ministry." But I am not trying to suggest that such works are lesser or that they do not foster the coming reign of God; rather, I am suggesting that ministry operates outside the sphere of intimacy.

I have already suggested that not every good work is ministry. Parents (and parent figures) nurture, guide, and protect children to heroic degrees. They sacrifice and commit themselves for the good of their children day after day in countless ways. That loving service may be a model for ministry, but I would not label it "ministry." It does not need to be subsumed under ministry, so great is it in itself. Visiting a friend or relative in the hospital is not ministry. It is what loving friends and relatives owe one another. Visiting in the name of the parish is another thing altogether. It is expanding a personal circle of intimacy to include others. It is a *public* act done in the name of the church.

Nor do I include praying as ministry. Prayer has its own wonderful impact and meaning, and our world and church would be destitute without it.

The intercessory prayers at Sunday Mass remind us of the obligation we have to pray for the church and for the world, especially those who suffer poverty and oppression. Only after we have prayed for the greater human and Christian community are we invited to offer our personal intentions. Prayer should be a regular part of a minister's life so that her or his ministry will be firmly rooted in God and carried out with compassion and courage, but prayer itself is not ministry. Prayer is the life blood that keeps our relationship with God thriving. It is necessary for us as individuals and as Christian ministers.

Perhaps we have too exalted an idea about ministry, which leads us to think other Christian acts like prayer and fidelity to the responsibilities of our vocation are somehow not as sacred in themselves. Ministry is one way—a very significant way—but only one way of living out our relationship with God.

In Christ's Name

The second piece of O'Meara's definition of ministry states that it is action performed by a baptized follower of Jesus Christ. The word "ministry" is a particularly Christian word. The wondrous work of Jews, Muslims, and others facilitates what we Christians refer to as the coming of the reign of God. It is work carried out in love and in answer to a call from God, but, according to this definition, it is not ministry because it is not done in the name of Jesus Christ. This does not mean that the good works of non-Christians are in any way lesser than those done by Christians. Juan Luis Segundo speaks of the work of those who are not Christian in glowing terms.

Christ chose to add an essential aspect to his picture of the judgment: the general surprise. On the scene are people who never saw him, people who passed through history before his coming, people who did not know him during their lifetime either personally or through his church. So the vast majority of human beings will ask the question that Christ puts on their lips: "Lord, when did we see you and succor you, when did we pass you by?" His answer is that it matters little that they never met him. The merit of the things they did for other human beings, invested with love, reaches the God who is brother of all and brings them eternal life.[8]

The Oxford English Dictionary offers the following introduction to its definition of minister: "*minus* less, parallel in formation to the correlative *magister* Master." The minister does not serve in her or his own name but in the name of Christ and impelled by the Christian community, thus giving ministry its unique Christian character. As we have already noted, ministry, as used in a religious sense, is a particularly Christian word. A minister is one who comes in the name of another; ministers come in the name of the risen Christ. Ministers, ordained or lay, do not minister in their own name, or for their own benefit or because of some generalized feeling of good will toward their fellow human beings. To minister is to make a deliberate and conscious decision to serve the community in the name of Christ. This is not to suggest that we need constantly to refer to this commitment. Rather, we need to renew it periodically, pray over it often, and allow it to color all that we do.

Personal Qualities of Ministry

An interesting and sometimes overlooked element in O'Meara's definition of ministry is the phrase, "flowing from the Spirit's charism and an individual personality." Ministers are equipped, by virtue of God's gifts, including all that makes up one's personality, for the ministry to which they are called. God does not ask the impossible of us but prepares each one for the calling, the vocation issued by the Spirit. That means giving us the personal qualities necessary for the work.

New Testament Ministry

Scripture offers no blueprint for ministry today other than the assurance that God has blessed each community with the gifts necessary for that community. Paul's listing of the gifts in 1 Corinthians 12 is sharp witness to this. There are, we are told, "different gifts but the same Spirit, different ministries but the same Lord, different works but the same God who accomplishes all of them in everyone. To each person the manifestation of the Spirit is given for the common good."

It should come as no surprise, then, that there is no one pattern of ministry for all communities. The Acts of the Apostles and the epistles give a variety of descriptions of various communities, including Antioch, Jerusalem, Ephesus, Corinth, and Rome. In each case, the problems encountered in the building of community were addressed by establishing ministries to serve the local *ekklesia*. We read of the Twelve, apostles, prophets, teachers, evangelists, and others who led the people of God in living the Way. It appears that the needs of the community dictated the kinds of ministries that arose. The Spirit provided the gifts necessary.

There is no talk of "laity" as a group ranked below the "clergy." In fact, those words and concepts are absent in the New Testament. The expression *kleros*, from which we get "clergy" is used to denote the whole body of the Christian people, rather than to describe a part of the community set apart.[9]

The Church's Mission

All ministry flows from the mission of the church, which, of course, is none other than the mission of Jesus:

> The spirit of God has been given to me,
>   for God has anointed me.
> God has sent me to bring good news to the poor;
> to proclaim liberty to captives; and to the blind, new
>   sight,
> to set the downtrodden free
>   and to proclaim God's year of favor. (Luke 4:17–19)

To speak of the church's mission is to acknowledge that the church does not exist for itself. The church exists for the world. Richard McBrien writes: "The church exists not alongside the world but within the world, and not in domination over the world but as its servant."[10] The church is for the world, just as Jesus is.

The split between religious faith and so-called secular activities has been recognized as "among of the most serious errors of our age."[11] Involvement in social, political, and economic affairs need not distract from religious commitment but should rather grow out of it and enrich it. This does not suppose commitment to one or the other political party or social movement, but it does encourage participation of individual Christians and all of us together as church in affairs that affect the lives of people and all of creation.

Today's Ministry: Collaborative

As we look at the needs of the church today, it becomes obvious that we must learn to work together, that collaboration must be the hallmark of our ministry. In the survey I did for this book, I asked what practices and characteristics are common among effective ministers. Almost every reply stated the need for collaboration. A common theme was: "I need a team that shares my values and that both encourages and challenges me."…"I appreciate co-ministry, clergy and lay together, not ministering in isolation."

On the other hand, after describing ministers with whom she ministered as enthusiastic and passionate about ministry, one person wrote, "One of the challenges of working with effective ministers is that they are so busy being 'out there' with the people that they are not very good at building team with the ministers around them."

Collaborative ministry is not easy. It is not about making us feel good about ourselves or what we do. While it presumes a warm relationship, it is not about becoming best friends.

Collaboration requires humility and honesty.

SUMMARY

1. Baptism and confirmation are sacraments of ministry. Holy Orders is the sacrament of a specific ministry within the Christian community.

2. Vatican II states that through baptism and confirmation we are called to ministry by the Lord himself.

3. Ministry has been described as *general universal* (that service to which all human beings are called), *general specific* (defined by special talent or train-

ing), *Christian universal* (that to which all Christians are called), and *Christian specific* (defined by special talent or training).

4. Thomas O'Meara has described Christian ministry as "the public activity of a baptized follower of Jesus Christ flowing from the Spirit's charism and an individual personality on behalf of the Christian community to witness, serve, and realize the Kingdom of God."

5. Ministry flows from the mission of the church, which is none other than the mission of Jesus.

6. Ministry today is marked by a spirit of collaboration, laity and clergy working together in mutual support and respect.

POINTS FOR REFLECTION

How would you define ministry? How can we recognize and support the gifts of parishioners for ecclesial ministry?

What can be done to help people understand the baptismal call to ministry in the particular circumstances of their lives?

Does your staff/team wish to embrace a collaborative style of ministry? If so, what steps need to be taken?

What adjectives might parishioners use to describe the ministry available to them? Your next parish survey might contain such a question.

CHAPTER SEVEN

Spirituality
of the Minister

"Spirituality"evokes visions of convents, monasteries, chapels, and churches. It conjures up images of saints praying and monks meditating. That may be a good starting point for a discussion of spirituality, but it is only a beginning. When John Cardinal Newman was asked what the word spirituality meant, he said it included getting up in the morning, saying prayers, having breakfast, going to work, and all the rest of daily activities.

What Newman was suggesting is that our relationship to God colors, and is colored by, all the events of life. What we call spirituality is too great to fit only in the chapel. Spirituality is shorthand for the way we relate to God, to one another, and to all of creation. This, of course, is not to deny the significance of prayer but rather to put prayer in conversation with the rest of our lives.

In this chapter we will reflect on the spirituality of the minister; that is, how we relate to God in the various aspects of life. Of course, this means finding God in the ministerial service that fills our days, but it also means finding God in family and friends and in all of creation. Christian spirituality is shorthand for this relationship with God and God's creation. I would suggest that keeping a Sabbath and maintaining joy are very good ways of fostering a deep spirituality.

Sharing God's Life

Each minute of the day is sacred, an opportunity to share in the very life of God. Time is so precious a gift that it is given to us in very small increments, lest we be overwhelmed by the exquisite magnificence of it. Henri Nouwen reminds us that "God is a God of the present. God is always in the moment, be that moment hard or easy, joyful or painful."[1]

Recognizing God in the moment, in every moment, does not mean walking around with our head in the clouds. Recognizing God in the moment involves developing an attitude toward life that is joyous and grateful. It also means not getting lost in the past or the future. Guilt and regret about the past and worry about the future blind us to the presence of God with and for us at each moment. God saturates this world every moment. Michael Morwood expresses that truth thus:

> If God is truly present everywhere, we should expect God's presence and something of God's nature to be revealed in all of creation. We should expect and take seriously that God's presence, God's spirit, has been and is at

work in all people, in all places, at all times, in a multitude of differing cultures, thought patterns, and worldviews.[2]

God is not some solitary being who dwells somewhere up there in heaven. God is incarnated in creation. "God does not operate as an outsider, distant from us. In fact, God cannot be elsewhere and not here at the same time. God can never be absent."[3]

The American workaholic culture suggests that only time spent in work is valuable. Genesis, on the other hand, tells a different story. God rested. There is no suggestion of work-related stress in the creation of the universe. There was no rush, no anxiety about how things would turn out. God created and then rested.

It seems to be an occupational hazard that ministers never seem to think that they have done enough. I do not know any ministers who are lazy or slothful or cutting back on the job. On the contrary, ministers often are expert workaholics. Ask yourself, "Is there time for rest and relaxation in my life? Is there time for family and friends? Is there time for talking with God?" More important, "Is there time for listening to God?"

Finding God in Ministry

Mark records that when Jesus was sending the Twelve out on mission, he gave them very specific instructions. "Take nothing on the journey" but a walking stick—no food, no traveling bag, not a coin in the purses on their belts. They were also instructed not to bring a change of clothes. They were, however, to wear sandals. What can this message mean for us today? I think if Jesus were around today, he might say something like, "Take good care of yourself (wear sandals), but you really don't need a computer, a VCR, or the newest line of religious books and films." Wonderful as these things are and helpful as they may be for the work we do, they do not touch the essence of what is needed for ministry. What we have to give is God, who dwells within us; we have the gift of ourselves, and the God who dwells within.

The sixth chapter of Mark tells us a bit about what it means to follow Jesus. The scenes described jump from the hubbub of ministering to crowds of people, to the need to get away, to then go back to the crowds, and then once more to go back to some solitude.

When the disciples returned, they were ecstatic about all they had done and taught; in the same way, we often rejoice at our experiences in ministry. Jesus advised them to take some time by themselves to think about the things that had happened. He knew they needed time to digest and understand what was happening. They did try—and perhaps they were able to talk it over out there in the middle of the lake. They must have taken their time crossing because the people walking around the lake arrived before them. Immediately Jesus began to teach, and then the apostles had to begin ministering again, feeding the five thousand who were seated (as the New American Bible reports) "neatly arranged like flower beds." After the people gathered up the leftovers, perhaps taking doggy bags home with them, Jesus "insisted that his disciples get back into the boat." He himself went off to a mountain to pray, but he created a place for the disciples to have some time for themselves.

Then a storm threatened the apostles, and Jesus came to them saying, "Get hold of yourselves! It is I. Do not be afraid." We are told that they did not understand about the loaves and fishes. In fact, "Their minds were completely closed to the meaning of the events."

Hustle and bustle, then solitude, more hustle and bustle, more solitude, and then a storm. Isn't this the pattern of ministry sometimes? It seems to me that ministers are sometimes caught up in the hustle and bustle and storms and don't get enough time away in the boat. I believe that too many of us don't see time to get away by oneself as an essential part of the life of a minister.

Sometimes, it seems, so many problems arise in one day that ministers run from one to the other, putting out fires, as it were, when their energy might be better spent looking for the arsonist. Of course, the problems of the day need to be attended to, but we must also concern ourselves about the root of the problems. That translates into moving from a reactive mode to a proactive one, and that, in turn, means building time for reflection into each day. Thinking, planning, analyzing, evaluating, reflecting prayerfully, while not usually written into a job description, are (or ought to be) major elements in a minister's day, and they should be scheduled, as are other important events.

The Minister as Prophet

The Catholic penchant for "both/and" rather than "either/or" leads me to insist that rootedness in the community and response to its concerns must be enhanced by a prophetic stance that helps to move the community to greater fidelity to the demands of Christ. Prophetic ministers help people to see what they might rather ignore. Prophets in our midst see what most of us are blind to. They are able to make connections between everyday events and the challenge of our religious beliefs.

Ministers serve the community as prophets when they are not so far ahead of the community as to be out of touch with it, or so deeply rooted in it as to be blind to its faults and failures. Serving in a prophetic way demands courage. Because they challenge the community to make difficult decisions, prophets are rarely popular. Serving in a prophetic way also demands humility. There is a danger of insisting on one's own way that is only reined in by a humble acceptance of advice from respected persons and by measuring each idea against the teaching of Jesus.

The prophet is able to see the suffering of people that is often missed by others. Empty bellies and empty hearts can blind people to what is offered by the parish. Lack of awareness of the pressures faced by people may result in the parish offering what is not needed or wanted. It may be better for us to spend some time on the issues—economic, political, and cultural—that concern parishioners' lives than on why fewer people come to Mass on Sunday or why the teenage program limps along. We might better consider the problems that overwhelm families so that we might put parish resources and talent at the service of those problems. It may be that the way the Eucharist is celebrated does not provide the spiritual nourishment that parishioners need. It may be that parish programs for teenagers are not welcoming and supportive of some youngsters.

Finding God in Loved Ones

Ministry is so fulfilling, so challenging, so energizing that it sometimes consumes more of our lives than it ought. As Melannie Svoboda, SND, notes, "It should come as no surprise that good-hearted people do fall prey to worka-holism, because workaholism can look a lot like dedica-tion!"[4] To be involved with a parish committed to the gospel, to work with and for people stumbling toward God, to feel that what we are doing with our life is worth-while—what could be more intoxicating?

That intoxication may blind us to other, more basic reali-ties in our lives. That blindness may be described as a sco-toma, an area of darkness in an otherwise healthy vision field. We may see most things in a balanced way but are unable to identify our ministry as intrusive in other areas of life. Feeling good about ourselves and what we do is often interpreted as virtue: "See how much I sacrifice for the mission!"

A friend of mine[5] found herself being deluged by demands of an already demanding ministry and sat herself down for some serious reflection. She came to the decision to make a "preferential option" for her children. All her deci-sions have to pass through the test of how they will affect her children, just as the social justice documents of the church commit it to make decisions in the light of their effect on the poor. It is her way of keeping first things first in her life.

Flannery O'Connor's writing is too dark for some peo-ple, but it has also been described as going to the bone of truth; perhaps that is what makes it so dark. In her stories the self-righteous person is often brought to a tragic end. This is nowhere more obvious than in "The Lame Shall Enter First,"[6] a short story in which O'Connor introduces Shepherd, father of Norton and benefactor-par-excellence to a lame boy named Rufus Johnson. Norton is a cause of dismay for his father; he is clumsy, messes things up, and generally acts like the ten-year-old that he is. He sorely misses his mother, who has died recently. Shepherd's frustration toward his son and his overwhelming generosity to Johnson are in sharp contrast. In Shepherd's eyes, his son can do no right; Johnson can do no wrong, even in spite of strong evidence to the contrary.

Johnson insults Shepherd and steals from him and from neighbors; Shepherd understands, because the boy has had a hard life. Johnson refuses the orthopedic shoes that Shepherd had specially made for him so he could walk better; he abuses Norton and teaches him to despise his father. No matter what Rufus Johnson does, Shepherd is sure that his love and generosity will be strong enough to effect a change in the child: "I'm stronger than you are. I'm stronger than you are and I'm going to save you. The good will triumph."

Finally, when Shepherd realizes that he has failed with Johnson, he says, "I have nothing to reproach myself with. I did more for him than I did for my own son." As he repeats the phrase, he realizes "he had stuffed his own emptiness with good works like a glutton.... His image of himself shriveled until everything was black before him." In typical O'Connor fashion, Shepherd's final punishment is the suicide of his son.

When I read this short story recently, I wondered if O'Connor chose the name "Shepherd" because she saw the way many shepherds, in their striving to do good works, lose sight of what is of great importance—the responsibilities that God has put into their lives in their families. Is it possible that we sometimes reserve our best behavior for the people with whom we minister but neglect to offer the same graciousness to our families?

If workers in a factory or office were frequently asked to work two or three hours extra in the evening without remuneration, local church officials would certainly side with the hapless workers in their struggle for justice. But when a parish minister is expected to attend or conduct evening sessions after a full day of ministry, justice considerations are often forgotten; the minister is expected to attend and perhaps conduct the evening session and then show up bright and shiny the next morning. I am not suggesting that this is done out of any meanness or exploitation; rather, it is because ministers are so zealous that they do not weigh what they do or ask other ministers to do with the same scales as they use for other people. Svoboda is right. Workaholism can look like dedication.

We might broaden the gospel injunction, "What does it profit a person to gain the whole world and lose their soul?" to "What does it profit ministers to gain the whole parish, and lose their loved ones?" When the demands, especially the time demands of ministry, threaten family or community life, we might wonder the reason. Is ministry being used to avoid family or community problems or is ministry getting in the way and causing problems in the family or community?

Friendship a Must

As I have already mentioned, so many of the ideas for this book came from ministers whom I respect and who shared their wisdom with me. During one conversation, we discussed our ideas about the characteristics of a good minister. After speaking of God, prayer, and reflection, we made a strong case for friendship. The group agreed that the inability to maintain intimate friendships was a red flag for ministry.

All relationships tend toward friendship. Grown children who maintain the same kind of relationship with their parents that saw them through childhood, spouses who are not also good friends, siblings who have not developed the love of friendship—all are unhealthy and unholy relationships. Parental love, marital love, and familial love all find their fulfillment in friendship. So, when I speak of friends, I include all those relationships. Friendship is so foundational, says Elizabeth Johnson that "the love of friendship is the very essence of God."[7] God, in God's very Being, is relational, is love, is friendship. The symbol of the Trinity is a profound way of expressing this mystery of relatedness. To be in relationship is to be Godlike.

Friends reveal us to ourselves in ways both surprising and disconcerting. We come to know ourselves through the good grace of friends. Friendship is the mature, trusting, mutual, and giving relationship that enables each one to be transformed into whom the friend sees and loves. It is a relationship that calls us to growth, that fosters the best in us, and that challenges us to holiness.

Friendship is that name we give to relationships of intimacy but not all intimacy is friendship. There is a hierarchy of intimacy, and friendship is the summit.[8] We can talk about physical intimacy—not sexual intimacy, but the kind of bodily communication that we do all the time. Just notice a newly engaged couple or really good friends in a crowd. They often signal one another and tell a whole story by exchanging a simple look. Of course, that eye communication is also used in more negative ways when signals of boredom or frustration or disdain are passed between persons.

Healing Touch

In different cultures, people stand closer or further away from one another, and the signals given by the distance are óften misread in multicultural situations. In our culture, women are freer than men in hugging and kissing one another. On a football field, men hug and touch one another in ways that might cause a fight elsewhere.

Recent sexual scandals and our growing awareness of the abuse of children have raised serious questions about appropriate touch in ministry. Teachers, counselors, and ministers are wary about touching lest they be misunderstood. The tenor of the times necessitates prudence, and yet the healing power of touch is so evident in the gospel stories. Repeatedly we are told that Jesus touched someone in need and they were healed. He stretched out his hand to the leper, took Peter's mother-in-law by the hand, and touched the eyes of the blind men. The hemorrhaging woman did not fear to touch him, and when he raised Jairus' daughter, he took her by the hand and said, "Talitha, koum," that is, "Little girl, get up."

A few medical schools have begun to teach the art of healing hands to students, whose touch will be so vital to patients. Ministers, too, are called on to learn that delicate distinction between healing hands and threatening ones. One of the sadnesses of our time is that so many children are growing up with skin hunger because those who love them are fearful of hugging them. Stories are still told of babies who die from lack of TLC and of elderly patients in nursing homes who are withering away from skin starvation.

Intellectual Intimacy

Some people who might never be able to demonstrate physical intimacy are able to become intellectually intimate. They are able to share profound ideas and concepts, and even hopes and dreams, and in so doing reveal the mystery of who they are and so invite others into a more intimate relationship.

The need for intimacy among human beings is so critical that as the communal ties of an earlier, less mobile time faded, churches began to establish prayer groups and Scripture study groups. The proliferation of small Christian communities and the wide variety of support groups in society remind us of the need for intimacy. Participants may never become best friends, and they may not get to know one another in a more deeply emotional or spiritual way, but some complexity of the human person is revealed, some vision of what matters in life is shared. This intellectual coming together is a form of intimacy.

On one level, intellectual intimacy supports a structure of inequality (for want of a better word). When hurting people come to a parish for assistance, material or spiritual, this is the kind of intimacy we often establish—warm, welcoming, understanding, but not revelatory of what our deepest concerns are. Our responsibility is getting to know others so that we may better serve their needs; but we do not necessarily let ourselves be known. That said, let me underscore that we always reveal who we are as we interact with people.

Cocktail party chatter is a superficial form of intellectual intimacy. It is a way of interacting, exchanging ideas, and maintaining conversation so as not to let ourselves be known. Classroom interactions, listening to lectures, taking notes, and regurgitating information at test time are other forms of superficial intimacy. Unfortunately, some church situations are conducive to keeping people apart. When people are known primarily by the roles they play in the community and by the titles they hold, anything but superficial intellectual intimacy is difficult.

Ministers need to be accessible to those in need, welcoming and accepting everyone, especially those who may be most difficult to accept. Often ministers are the only ones in some persons' lives who treat them with understanding and compassion. No wonder some grow to depend on their ministers and even misunderstand some of our ministerial overtures as invitations to friendship.

On the other side of the ledger are those ministers who find their friends only among those to whom they minister. In such cases, it is difficult to maintain a relationship of mutuality. Ministers are already (by virtue of their role) in a dominant position and therefore not as vulnerable. For ministers who find themselves without friends except those they help and heal, I would suggest a long talk with a spiritual director or counselor.

Good fences make good neighbors, and good boundaries make good ministers. All of this is not to suggest that we ministers should not be friendly and warm; only that we should not seek emotional fulfillment from those to whom we minister. The ministerial relationship may be described as one of "temporary dependence," as I described in chapter three. Permanent dependence, you may recall, is for the benefit of the more powerful partner in the relationship; the slave-master relationship is perhaps the most dramatic example. Temporary dependence, on the other hand, is for the benefit of the person in need, and the whole purpose of the relationship is to eliminate the imbalance.

Doctors serve patients to bring them to health and to end the need for the medical visits. Teachers strive to bring students to intellectual maturity and to become unnecessary in student's lives. Parents are in business to make themselves obsolete. (Please understand that I am not talking here about a rejection of parenthood, only that healthy relationships between parents and adult children ordinarily become less dependent and more mutual.)

The point of the ministerial relationship is to bring the people of God to full maturity. That means working ourselves out of a job by creating more ministers.

Sabbath

God rested on the seventh day. After a week of work creating this universe, separating land and water, flinging birds into the air and fish into the sea, of setting us in the midst of all the grandeur, God rested. Genesis tells us not only that God rested but commands that we are to rest also, to keep the Lord's Day holy.

Imagine! The day identified as the Lord's Day is a day of rest, not a day of hard work or of penance. The major religions all identify a day where work shall cease. Jews still celebrate Sabbath on the seventh day of the week, and Moslems celebrate it on Friday. For parish ministers, the Christian Sabbath is hardly a day of rest, but that ought not get in the way of our creating a sabbath on another day. It certainly ought not get in the way of creating small sabbaths, often during the week—moments to cherish and share with friends, moments to recoup energy, moments to refresh one's spirit.

Maria Harris has done much to restore our sense of sabbath. She reminds us:

> Unfortunately, religious institutions and religious officials have often so overcontrolled the Sabbath with man-made rules and regulations, in contrast to divine law that the essential note is forgotten: it is a *commandment to rest*. The Sabbath is a commandment that tells us not only what to do, it is a *commandment that tells us what to be*. We are the beings in creation who rest. We are the beings who have a divine law within us—a law that says to us, "Periodically, you must rest, you must dwell, you must turn from the creating of the world to its Creator."[9]

That Your Joy May be Full

Given the sacramental character of the Catholic Church, it would seem that joy and thanksgiving would mark our every relationship but especially that relationship we call ministry. The Vatican II document in which the church discusses its relationship with the world is aptly titled *Gaudium et Spes* (Joy and Hope). This is not naive jollity but the deep and profound joy and hope that arise from our firm belief that God is truly in love with us. God loves us so much that God wants to spend eternity with us. Because we are a sacramental people, we are able to recognize this loving God in all things—weddings and funerals, welcomes and good-byes, sicknesses and health, wealth and poverty. How could we not be joyful?

It is hard to miss biblical writers' attention to the virtue of joy. Mentioned in the occasion of the deliverance of the Hebrews by Esther, repeated in the psalms and the prophets, it marks the beginning and the end of the gospels of Matthew and Luke. John sings of it, and Paul mentions it dozens of times.

The magi were filled with joy at seeing the star that would lead them to the Christ Child (Mt 2:10). The angel tells Zechariah, the Baptizer's father that John will be filled with joy (Lk 1:14). The babe in Elizabeth's womb leapt for joy at Mary's greeting (Lk 1:44). The shepherds hear the song of the angels bringing tidings of great joy (Lk 2:10).

During the public life of Jesus, we hear of the joy upon one sinner's return (Lk 15:7) and the promise of joy to the servant who wisely invested the master's treasure (Mt 25:23). When the seventy-two disciples returned from their internship as ministers, they expressed their joy that the demons were subject to them (Lk 10:17).

And finally, after the resurrection of Jesus, joy saturates the life of the disciples. Mary Magdalene and the other Mary hurried from the tomb in fear and great joy (Mt 28:8). The disciples were incredulous for sheer joy as Jesus convinced them that it was truly he (Lk 24:41), and they returned to Jerusalem (and possible martyrdom) filled with joy.

John repeatedly speaks of the followers of Jesus being full of joy. In his prayer for them at the Last Supper, Jesus prayed, "that they may share my joy completely" (Jn 17:13).

These insights into the kind of joy that Jesus promised should cure us of any misconception that this joy means delight, bliss, or gaiety. This joy is a deeper awareness of the "more than meets the eye" in the everyday events of life. It is the ability to see God, to recognize that holy presence in the happy and sad times, in the problems and in the solutions. This joy is more than quiet contentment; it involves faith and hope and love. This joy is a firm rootedness in God; it is sharing in God's life.

It should be obvious that I am not making a case for Catholic Polyannas walking around with their heads in the clouds, oblivious of the pain and sorrow that fill so many persons' lives. The profound joy of which I speak serves to open hearts to the plight of suffering people, in charity and in justice. It is the kind of joy apparent in the life of Dorothy Day,[10] in spite of her immersion in the poverty, pain, and degradation of others.

C.S. Lewis describes a search for Joy (always capitalized by him as if to give us a hint of what he was searching for) that led him from the Christianity of his childhood, through atheism, to a more mature and stunning appropriation of Christianity. He describes his futile attempts and vain hopes to capture Joy as "merely the mental track left by the passage of Joy—not the wave but the imprint of the wave upon the sand."[11] Lewis, like so many of us, mistook clues and hints about Joy for Joy itself. Hearing Wagner, reading the Norse and Celtic mythologies, finding a first friend, pursuing academic delights all gave him a stab of Joy but all were only the image or sensation of Joy, not Joy itself. He says, "all images and sensations, if idolatrously mistaken for Joy itself, soon honestly confessed themselves inadequate. All said, in the last resort, 'It is not I. I am only a reminder. Look! Look! What do I remind you of?'"

Joy is the appropriate response to our belief that God created us in love and wills only love for us. Joy is our human response for this lavish divine love. Joy is the gift of this lavish divine love.

SUMMARY

1. The word "spirituality" refers to how we relate to God, to others, to all of creation, and to self in the dailiness of our lives.

2. God saturates the world. God is in every moment whether hard or easy, delightful or painful.

3. Some ministers tend to be workaholics. There is a need to find time for rest, relaxation, and play, but especially time for God, for family, and for friends.

4. Time for reflection belongs on every minister's daily schedule.

5. Ministers are sometimes called to serve the community as prophet, enabling them to see and respond to evils in society that may be being ignored.

6. Relationships developed in ministry are meant to bring persons to full Christian maturity, not to make them dependent on us.

7. We are commanded to keep a Sabbath and thereby acknowledge that we leave all in the hands of God.

POINTS FOR REFLECTION

In what ways might you mistake workaholism for dedication?

What reminders of God's abiding presence might you build into your day?

Review your appointment book. What times in each day might you block out for prayer and reflection? for a mini-sabbatical?

Make a list of persons who enrich your life with the gift of friendship. How might those relationships mirror the relationship enjoyed by the Trinity?

Since Sunday is usually a busy day for parish ministers, how do you manage to keep holy the Lord's Day?

Notes

Chapter One: Fostering Faith

1. Sharon Parks in *To Act Justly, Love Tenderly, Walk Humbly* by Walter Brueggemann, Sharon Parks, Thomas Groome (New York: Paulist Press, 1986), 30.
2. Walter Bruggemann in *To Act Justly, Love Tenderly, Walk Humbly,* 26.
3. Richard McBrien, *Catholicism* (San Francisco: HarperCollins, 1994), 22.
4. Avery Dulles, *The Survival of Dogma* (New York: Crossroad Publishing Co., 1982), 138.
5. Sallie McFague, *The Body of God* (Minneapolis: Fortress Press, 1993), 67.

Chapter Two: Imaging God

1. Joyce Rupp, O.S.M., "Rediscovering God in the Midst of Our Work," in *Handbook of Spirituality for Ministers,* edited by Robert Wicks (New York: Paulist Press, 1995), 272.
2. Catherine LaCugna, *God for Us* (San Francisco: Harper, 1991), 243.
3. LaCugna, *God for Us,* 322.
4. Sara Maitland, *Big Enough God* (New York: Henry Holt, 1995), 5.
5. Elizabeth Johnson, *She Who Is* (New York: Crossroad Publishing Co., 1992), 199-200.
6. LaCugna, *God for Us,* 382-83.
7. New Testament scholar Mary Rose D'Angelo suggests barley, the grain of the first harvest, was probably the grain commonly used for bread at the time of Passover in Jesus' time. Wheat was one of the more fragile grains available at later harvests. Conversation 2/25/01.

8. Joanmarie Smith, *Teaching as Eucharist* (Mineola NY: Resurrection Press, 1999), 16.

Chapter Three: Coming to Know Christ

1. Elizabeth A. Johnson, *Consider Jesus* (New York: Crossroad Publishing Co., 1990), 30.
2. Kenan B. Osborn, *Ministry* (Mahwah N.J.: Paulist Press, 1995), 71.
3. LaCugna, *God for Us,* 407.
4. Dorothy Day, *The Long Loneliness* (New York: Harper and Row, 1952).
5. Jean Baker Miller, *Toward a New Psychology of Women* (Boston: Beacon Press, 1976), 4-12.
6. Robert Krieg, *Story Shaped Christology* (New York: Paulist Press, 1988), 112-113.
7. Quoted by Doris Jean Dyke in *Crucified Woman* (Toronto: The United Church Publishing House, 1991), 42.

Chapter 4: To Be Human

1. Johnson, *Consider Jesus,* 21-25.
2. Anne Frank, *Diary of a Young Girl* (New York: Random House, 1952), 184.
3. Richard McBrien, *Ministry* (San Francisco: Harper and Row, 1987), 59.
4. Augustine, *Confessions* X, 27.
5. Andrew Greeley, "The Apologetics of Beauty" *America,* September 16, 2000.
6. Johnson, *Consider Jesus,* 24.
7. Karl Rahner, S.J., *The Rahner Reader* (New York: Crossroad Publishing Co., 1984), 185.
8. Boff, Leonardo, *Liberating Grace* (Maryknoll, NY: Orbis Books, 1979), 137.

9. Day, *The Long Loneliness,* 89.

10. *Gandhi on Christianity,* edited by Robert Ellsberg (Maryknoll, NY: Orbis Books, 1991), 37.

11. See John 11:5 for the surprising statement, "Jesus loved Martha and her sister (not named) and Lazarus very much."

12. Paul Mundey, *Unlocking Church Doors* (Nashville, TN: Abingdon Press, 1997), 43-50.

13. Quoted in Mundey, *Unlocking Church Doors,* 50.

Chapter 5: Church

1. Eugene Maly, *The Priest in Sacred Scripture* (Washington, DC: United States Catholic Conference, 1972).

2. Karl Rahner, "A Fundamental Theological Interpretation of Vatican II" in *Vatican II: The Unfinished Agenda* edited by Lucien Richard, O.M.I., and Daniel Harrington, S.J. (New York: Paulist Press, 1987), 14-15.

3. "Message to Humanity" in *The Documents of Vatican II* edited by Walter M. Abbott, S.J. (New York: America Press, 1966), 5.

4. Walbert Buhlmann, O.F.M. Cap., *The Coming of the Third Church* (Maryknoll, NY: Orbis Press, 1978).

5. Elie Wiesel, *The Night Trilogy* (New York: Hill and Wang, 1997) 71-72.

6. Hilaire Belloc quoted in *I Like Being a Catholic* edited by Michael Leach and Therese Borchard (New York: Doubleday, 2000), 115.

7. Elizabeth Johnson, *Friends of God and Prophets* (New York: Continuum, 1998) 8.

8. Johnson, *Friends of God and Prophets,* 220.

Chapter 6: Who Are Called to Minister?

1. Walter M. Abbott, S.J., *The Documents of Vatican II* (New York: The America Press, 1966), 775.

2. *The Laity, Called and Gifted* (Washington, D.C.: United States

Catholic Conference, 1980), 8.

3. *The Laity, Called and Gifted,* 12.

4. *Called and Gifted for the Third Millennium* (Washington, D.C.: United States Catholic Conference, 1995), 24.

5. See Richard McBrien, *Ministry: A Theological Pastoral Handbook* (San Francisco: Harper and Row, 1987).

6. McBrien, *Ministry: A Theological Pastoral Handbook,* 12. Italics in the original.

7. Thomas O'Meara, *Theology of Ministry* (New York: Paulist Press, 1999), 150.

8. Juan Luis Segundo, S.J., *The Community Called Church* (Maryknoll, N.Y.: Orbis Books, 1973), 9-10.

9. See Alexandre Faivre, *The Emergence of the Laity in the Early Church* (Mahwah, N.J.: Paulist Press, 1990) especially Chapter 1, "The wonderful time when there was neither clergy nor laity" and Edward Schillebeeckx, *The Church With a Human Face* (New York: Crossroad, 1985) for an extended investigation of the life and ministry of the early church.

10. McBrien, *Ministry: A Theological Pastoral Handbook,* 672.

11. *Gaudium et Spes,* n. 43.

Chapter Seven: Spirituality of the Minister

1. Henri Nouwen, *Here and Now: Living in the Spirit* (New York: Crossroad, 1994), 18.

2. Michael Morwood, M.S.C., *Tomorrow's Catholic: Understanding God and Jesus in a New Millennium* (Mystic, CT: Twenty-Third Publications, 1999), 47.

3. Morwood, *Tomorrow's Catholic,* 46.

4. Melannie Svoboda, S.N.D., *Traits of a Healthy Spirituality* (Mystic, CT: Twenty-Third Publications, 1996), 106.

5. Kathryn Schneider, in a conversation in the Fall of 1998.

6. Flannery O'Connor, "The Lame Shall Enter First," in *Everything That Rises Must Converge* (New York: Farrar, Straus and Giroux, 1972), 143-190.

7. Johnson, *She Who Is* (New York: Crossroad Publishing Company, 1992), 218.

8. Alan Dahms, *Emotional Intimacy: Overlooked Requirement for Survival* (Detroit: Wayne State University Press, 1972), 20-57.

9. Maria Harris, *Dance of the Spirit* (New York: Bantam, 1989), 92-93.

10. See Dorothy Day, *The Long Loneliness* (San Francisco: Harper and Row, 1952). Day's joy is evident in the ways she describes the events of her life, especially the gracious and generous way she introduces the people who shared those events.

11. C.S. Lewis, *Surprised by Joy* (New York: Harcourt Brace Jovanovich, 1984), 219.

Of Related Interest

The Total Parish Manual
Everything you Need to Empower Your Faith Community
William J. Bausch

The complete "how-to" for guiding a parish to fulfilling its mission to its members. Covers the sacraments, the liturgical year, volunteers, organizations, ministries, small faith communities, evangelization, and other parish activities.
0-89622-607-7, 328 pp, $29.95 (M-03)

A User-Friendly Parish
Becoming a More Welcoming Community
Judith Ann Kollar

The author points out some of the day-to-day elements in parish life that affect the way a parish functions and the way it is perceived by parishioners, visitors, and inquirers.
0-89622-937-8, 80 pp, $7.95 (C-10)

The I Like Being in Parish Ministry series
Each of these 48-page books offers practical advice as well as spiritual enrichment in a format that is clear and easy to use. Written by experienced authors who have long served in their particular ministries, these creative and informative books offer seasoned ministers a marvelous way to look deeper into their ministry and to develop a greater sense of how their service enriches both their lives and the lives of others. For those just beginning to serve in a particular ministry, these books will help lay the foundation for a rich and rewarding time of service. $4.95 each; bulk prices available.

Available for Presider, Assembly, Lector, Eucharistic Minister, Pastoral Council, Social Justice, Deacon, Catechist, DRE, and Youth Minister

Available at religious bookstores or from:
TWENTY-THIRD PUBLICATIONS
🌐 **A Division of Bayard** PO BOX 180 · MYSTIC, CT 06355
1-800-321-0411 · FAX: 1-800-572-0788 · E-MAIL: ttpubs@aol.com
www.twentythirdpublications.com
Call for a free catalog